TAKING THE LEAD

TAKING THE LEAD

FOLLOWING THE EXAMPLE OF PAUL, TIMOTHY, & SILVANUS

RON JENSON

Multnomah Publishers *Sisters, Oregon*

TAKING THE LEAD
published by Multnomah Publishers, Inc.

and in association with the literary agency of Alive Communications,
1465 Kelly Johnson Blvd., Suite 320, Colorado Springs, CO 80920

© 1998 by Ron Jenson
International Standard Book Number: 1-57673-254-1

Cover photograph by Robert Holmgren/Tony Stone Images

Printed in the United States of America

For information:
MULTNOMAH PUBLISHERS, INC.
POST OFFICE BOX 1720
SISTERS, OREGON 97759

98 99 00 01 02 03 04 05 — 10 9 8 7 6 5 4 3 2 1

I dedicate this book to some of the men who have joined so many great women in providing a model of leadership for me:

- Robert Jenson, my dad and friend — the most gentle man I know
- Matt Jenson, my son and friend — my model of integrity
- Dick Jenson, my big brother and friend — my teammate who always treated me as special

- Kevin Jenkins, my friend — the epitome of discipline
- Bob Safford, my friend — proof of the blessings of hard work

- Doug Tucker, my business partner and friend — a standout at dealing with issues head-on
- Bill Bright, my spiritual mentor and friend — my model for spiritual intimacy and holiness
- Alan Hlavka, my spiritual son and friend — the most earnest man I've ever met

- Dennis Rainey, my friend — my example of godly passion
- Ray Bentley, my pastor and friend — a servant leader, communicator, and friend

- Dick Ormsby, my neighbor and friend — a man of affection and not afraid to show it

- Grant Howard, my professor and friend — the best teacher on transparency I could imagine

- Howard Hendricks, my mentor and friend — the most effective communicator I know

Acknowledgments

"The body of Christ is knit together by that which every joint and ligament supplies," said the apostle Paul. Every part has to work together.

The same thing is true in writing a book.

I came up with the idea, taught this content to many groups of men over the years, then put it into print. Mary, my wife, edited, sharpened, and honed my work (as she always does). Dan Benson, senior editor of Christian living books at Multnomah, put his arms around my rough concepts and made powerful suggestions for improvement. (I didn't like some of them at first but I needed to hear them.) Then Jean Bryant took the manuscript and gave it a spit polish. (I don't think she actually spit on it, but you get my drift.)

All the time this was going on, Don Jacobson, publisher of Multnomah, was working with his team to be sure this work could be packaged, printed, marketed, and sold. Then all those media outlets, bookstores, and other distribution channels went to work. You see—the body of Christ at work on a book project. To all these people I say, thank you! The Multnomah team is an absolute delight.

Now all that's left is for you to read this book, like it, and buy 732 copies for your closest friends…and the work will be complete.

Contents

The Making of a Christian Leader

¹ For you yourselves know, brethren, that our coming to you was not in vain,

² but after we had already suffered and been mistreated in Philippi, as you know, we had the boldness in our God to speak to you the gospel of God amid much opposition.

³ For our exhortation does not come from error or impurity or by way of deceit;

⁴ but just as we have been approved by God to be entrusted with the gospel, so we speak, not as pleasing men but God, who examines our hearts.

⁵ For we never came with flattering speech, as you know, nor with a pretext for greed—God is witness—

⁶ nor did we seek glory from men, either from you or from others, even though as apostles of Christ we might have asserted our authority.

⁷ But we proved to be gentle among you, as a nursing mother tenderly cares for her own children.

⁸ Having thus a fond affection for you, we were well-pleased to impart to you not only the gospel of God but also our own lives, because you had become very dear to us.

⁹ For you recall, brethren, our labor and hardship, how working night and day so as not to be a burden to any of you, we proclaimed to you the gospel of God.

¹⁰ You are witnesses, and so is God, how devoutly and uprightly and blamelessly we behaved toward you believers;

¹¹ just as you know how we were exhorting and encouraging and imploring each one of you as a father would his own children,

¹² so that you may walk in a manner worthy of the God who calls you into His own kingdom and glory.

1 Thessalonians 2:1–12

A Psalm of Life

What the Young Man Said to the Psalmist

Tell me not, in mournful numbers,
Life is but an empty dream!
For the soul is dead that slumbers
And things are not what they seem.

Life is real! Life is earnest!
And the grave is not its goal;
Dust thou art, to dust returnest,
Was not spoken of the soul.

Not enjoyment, and not sorrow,
Is our destined end or way;
But to act, that each to-morrow
Find us further than to-day.

Art is long, and Time is fleeting,
And our hearts, though stout and brave,
Still, like muffled drums, are beating
Funeral marches to the grave.

In the world's broad field of battle,
In the bivouac of Life,
Be not like dumb, driven cattle!
Be a hero in the strife!

Trust no Future, howe'er pleasant!
Let the dead Past bury its dead!
Act, act in the living Present!
Heart within, and God o'erhead!

Lives of great men all remind us
We can make our lives sublime,
And departing, leave behind us
Footprints on the sands of time.

Footprints, that perhaps another,
Sailing o'er life's solemn main,
A forlorn and shipwrecked brother,
Seeing, shall take heart again.

Let us, then, be up and doing,
With a heart for any fate;
Still achieving, still pursuing,
Learn to labor and to wait.

—HENRY WADSWORTH LONGFELLOW

CHAPTER ONE

CHRISTIAN MEN WANTED!

The Challenge We Face

What a week! *Pressure* summed it up in one word. By the end of that week, some years ago, the pressure had grown to overwhelming proportions. I wondered, *Where is the spiritually mature Christian man I thought I was?* Three snapshots from that week showed me I had plenty of homework to do if I really wanted to be that man.

Snapshot one: I had just finished my second week back as president of a Christian seminary after being away during the summer. I had barely begun to dig out from the accumulated mess when my board informed me I was to raise 1.5 million dollars during that school year. This fund-raising was to be juggled with my regular workload, writing a new seminary prospectus, and never-ending personnel problems. Each of these responsibilities carried its own share of pressure, and I was sure I would collapse when they fell on me all at once.

I shut my office door, took the phone off the hook, and reached for my Bible. I knew I needed help from God's Word or I wouldn't be able to cope. Somewhere in there God must have included instructions for Christian leadership. I needed to find those instructions and follow them.

Snapshot two: That same week I rushed home late from the office one night and got there just in time to host a Neighborhood Safety Watch meeting. I considered myself a conscientious Christian, concerned about people around me, but when I walked into my living room, I was shocked. About thirty of my neighbors were there, and after living three years in our cul-de-sac, I knew fewer than half of them.

Another pressure. I hadn't measured up to my own standard as a caring

Christian, much less the standard God provides through the example of Jesus Christ. I resolved that night to begin to genuinely care for my neighbors.

Snapshot three: That same week, Molly, my three-year-old daughter, was in the living room playing with her inflatable plastic arm cuffs. She had just begun swimming lessons, and her "swimmies" seemed to be her favorite toy. Her brother, Matt, who had just turned six and considered himself quite the adult, tried to help Molly put them on her arms. "Now, Molly," Matt said, "let me show you how to pull these up!"

He took one from her and she instantly let out an ear-piercing scream: "Gimme my swimmie!"

I hadn't been paying much attention to the children, but I heard Molly scream. Matt began yelling back at her, still clutching her swimmie. "Matthew," I demanded, "quit yelling and apologize to your sister. Right now!"

Matt dutifully apologized.

But Mary, my wife, had heard more of the argument than I had. She intervened and ordered Molly to apologize to Matt for her anger when he was only trying to help. Guilt clutched me—I had jumped all over Matt without knowing what was going on.

I got up, scooped him into my arms, and apologized. He took it better than I would have if someone had accused me and made me apologize for something that wasn't my fault.

Stress! I had to be a more effective father. How could I be a strong male role model for my children and yet still be fair and loving? The pressure I felt that day as a parent was perhaps the strongest of all. I determined to turn to God's Word, discover biblical parenting, and begin practicing it.

IDENTIFYING THE PROBLEM

I'm convinced my struggles are shared by most Christian men today. Many of my friends commiserate with me regularly about these common problems. During the last three years, though, I have seen my life transformed through the application of certain biblical principles. Beyond my own personal struggles, I have watched closely as Christian men increasingly seek to be the leaders God has called them to be. The phenomenal growth of Promise Keepers is a graphic illustration of this trend.

The good news is that men by the tens of thousands are coming to large stadium events and making commitments to be Promise Keepers. The bad news is that when they go home, they seldom find the needed training and support to sustain a changed life. New habits are begun but often not embedded into the lives of these men. The Promise Keepers leadership team, in an honest attempt to honor the local church, has assumed that such discipleship would take place through the church. Sometimes that happens. But sadly, this is the exception, not the rule.

The result is often frustration, discouragement, and a hardening of the heart. I have seen the problems firsthand at the thirty-plus Promise Keepers Leadership Seminars I have conducted in the U.S. and overseas. It's a serious dilemma and must be addressed in a life-changing, sustained way.

FINDING THE MOTIVATION

What about you? Have you made commitments at Promise Keepers events, a church service, a retreat, or any other type of meeting and then found yourself fighting to keep those commitments? If you have, welcome to the club. I want you to know you are just like the rest of us!

It is a lot easier to be a promise maker than a promise keeper. Believe me, I struggle with this daily. But remember, it is Satan, not Jesus, who wants to get you discouraged with your own frailties. He knows that if he can make you feel like a hypocrite he will win the battle.

Don't let the enemy do this. God has a plan for you—for a future and a hope. He not only wants you to be a promise keeper but a "promise reproducer." He really does.

God wants to use you to touch the lives of those around you: your family, your friends, the people in your church, the people at your job, and those in your community. If you can embrace the fact that God wants to use you, you will be more motivated to keep your promises and commitments.

It was through empathy with men like you and through my own struggles that my search for some core principles of leadership was born.

THREE ATTRIBUTES OF MATURITY

As I studied the Scriptures, I discovered that the healthiest church in the New Testament was the church at Thessalonica. This is the only church we read about in this time that manifested three vital attributes of maturity: faith, hope and love. Paul praises the church for its "work of faith and labor of love and steadfastness of hope" (1 Thessalonians 1:3). This church had it all!

First, the Thessalonians had *works of faith*. They didn't just talk about their faith, they lived it! Paul says they "turned to God from idols to serve a living and true God" (1 Thessalonians 1:9) and that from them the gospel went throughout the entire world. These people were movers.

What works of faith are you experiencing personally? What specific prayers has God answered recently? What miracles has He brought about in your life? I don't mean just physical healing (though God still is doing that). What relationships have been restored, finances provided, insights from the Word of God gained, new godly habits formed?

Second, these believers manifested a *labor of love.* This word *labor* comes from the concept of kneading bread. You must work the dough, which is hard work. So is love. The people of Thessalonica desperately loved one another. This wasn't a sentimental type of love. It was proactive and deliberate. They sacrificed to care for those around them. They met the needs of people and built a radical community of lovers who together manifested biblical unity.

The Thessalonians weren't just committed to unanimity (thinking the same) or uniformity (looking the same) or union (being in the same group). They displayed unity—a oneness of spirit. Don't get me wrong; they had their problems just like you and I have in our relationships. But they worked through their difficulties. They didn't deny them or let them become overwhelming. They dealt with them.

When they needed to weep with those who hurt, they wept. When they needed to admonish a deliberately sinful member, they did so. When they needed to care for the needy, they cared. In so doing, they built a unified body of believers known for their oneness of spirit, which is biblical unity.

How about you? How is your labor of love? Do you deal with conflicts appropriately and lovingly? Are you meeting the needs of your wife? Do your children get what they need? Do you radically love others in your church in a way that produces a spirit of unity visible to outsiders?

Third, they had a *steadfastness of hope.* Because they believed God, they knew He would work out any problems they had, so they didn't quit. They didn't give up in the midst of their trials or persecutions. They eagerly expected God to work it out.

How is your hope factor? Do you find yourself overwhelmed by the pressure around you? Are you a victim or a victor? How are you handling your stresses? Are you winning or losing? Are you coping or conquering in the midst of these challenges?

DEVELOPING THE ATTRIBUTES

If you struggle personally in your application of these three attributes of maturity (faith, hope, and love), you are, again, in good company. Look around your own home and church and determine how these qualities are revealed or are lacking. You see, we have lost sight of what God wants to do in and through us. So how do we get back in line?

We start by discovering what brought this transforming life into the church in Thessalonica. Why were these believers able to develop such a dynamic lifestyle? When we study the text carefully, we find that it had everything to do with the leadership of those who initially built the church.

Three men, Paul, Timothy, and Silvanus, moved into the city and spent several months pouring their lives into these people. Though very different from each other (Paul was the aggressive leader; Timothy, the timid teacher; and Silvanus, the servant administrator), these men all evidenced ten specific core leadership traits.

That is what made the difference in the church. It worked then—it works today! If you and I exercise these ten qualities consistently, we can see the same results in our homes, churches, businesses, and communities.

PAUL'S TEN CORE LEADERSHIP QUALITIES

As we journey through this book together, we will consider these ten leadership qualities—each of which can help us become more effective husbands and fathers, workers, and neighbors. They will provide a positive framework for the attitudes and actions we want to display. Take a few moments to carefully read the following passage from 1 Thessalonians. See if you can find the ten qualities that ought to be reflected in our lives.

> But we were gentle among you, like a mother caring for her little children. We loved you so much that we were delighted to share with you not only the gospel of God but our lives as well, because you had become so dear to us. Surely you remember, brothers, our toil and hardship; we worked night and day in order not to be a burden to anyone while we preached the gospel of God to you.
>
> You are witnesses, and so is God, of how holy, righteous and blameless we were among you who believed. For you know that we dealt with each of you as a father deals with his own children, encouraging, comforting and urging you to live lives worthy of God, who calls you into his kingdom and glory. (1 Thessalonians 2:7–12, NIV)

Did you spot them? Here are the ten core qualities I find:

CORE QUALITIES OF LEADERSHIP	
1	Team orientation, v. 8
2.	A disciplined life, v. 8
3.	Gentleness, v. 7
4.	The freedom to be affectionate, v. 8
5.	The ability to communicate effectively, v. 8
6.	Openness and honesty, vv. 8–9
7.	The desire to work hard, v. 9
8.	A willingness to serve, v. 9
9.	Holiness, v. 10
10.	The ability to confront, vv. 11–12

When we apply these ten biblical principles for Christian living to our own lives, we can become more and more the Christian men God wants us to be.

Action Steps

Go back to the section on faith, hope, and love and reflect on those questions with reference to your personal life, home, and church. Then evaluate yourself in this table (2 = weak performance and 10 = outstanding performance).

AREA OF LIFE	FAITH	HOPE	LOVE
Personal	2 4 6 8 10	2 4 6 8 10	2 4 6 8 10
Home	2 4 6 8 10	2 4 6 8 10	2 4 6 8 10
Business	2 4 6 8 10	2 4 6 8 10	2 4 6 8 10
Church	2 4 6 8 10	2 4 6 8 10	2 4 6 8 10

What one thing can you do this week to improve your own life in the areas of faith, hope, or love?

Evaluate your own life in light of the ten core qualities of leadership:

LEADERSHIP QUALITY	HOME	CHURCH	WORK
Team orientation	2 4 6 8 10	2 4 6 8 10	2 4 6 8 10
Disciplined life	2 4 6 8 10	2 4 6 8 10	2 4 6 8 10
Gentleness	↓2 4 6 8 10	2 4 6 8 10	2 4 6 8 10
Affection	↓2 4 6 8 10	2 4 6 8 10	2 4 6 8 10
Effective communication	2 4 6 8 10	2 4 6 8 10	2 4 6 8 10
Openness and honesty "help"	↓2 4 6 8 10	2 4 6 8 10	2 4 6 8 10
Desire to work hard	2 4 6 8 10	2 4 6 8 10	2 4 6 8 10 ↑ Thanks God!
Willingness to serve	2 4 6 8 10	2 4 6 8 10	2 4 6 8 10
Holiness	2 4 6 8 10	2 4 6 8 10	2 4 6 8 10
Ability to confront	2 4 6 8 10	2 4 6 8 10	2 4 6 8 10

Now identify one area where you are strong (e.g., hard work at business) and one area where you need to grow (e.g., affection at home). Thank God for that strength then commit to do one thing this week to strengthen your weakness. Write out the activity below and put it onto your calendar (listing when, where, and with whom you will do this).

Hard work, openess, gentleness + honesty in my Family — starting Now!

CHAPTER TWO

BUILDING
BIBLICAL BROTHERHOOD

Exposing the Need for Team

When was the last time you heard someone say, "Look out for number one" or "I don't need anyone"? That egocentric spirit seems to pervade our society today. Somehow we have concluded that the strong, powerful person is someone who doesn't need anyone else. Think of James Bond. Here is a tough, rugged, independent, distant, controlled man who takes things into his own hands. He doesn't need anyone. He is a loner who handles life by himself.

This isolationist spirit of our age was graphically illustrated to me one day in a restaurant. As I sat there, two men in softball uniforms came in with their wives. They were obviously obsessed with the softball league mania that hits every summer and were willing to give their free time to compete in every game during the season.

Their competitiveness excited my interest as they talked. They fought for the check, and I mean really fought for it! Each wanted to pay; each wanted to conquer and be the winner. They obviously liked one another but were careful not to show any open affection. I was so taken by how typically they acted that I approached them, told them I was writing a men's book, and asked them to contribute.

They both laughed nervously when I asked them to define a man. One of the men looked at his wife, who gave him a piercing glance. He said, "I don't know," as though any definition he came up with would not be acceptable to his wife.

But the other one said, "A man is a person who knows himself, has his own ideas and sticks to them, can take the good with the bad, and doesn't need anything."

There it was! A real man stands alone and doesn't need anything or anyone! That's the creed of our day. The ironic thing is that these two men, though they didn't realize it, desperately needed each other. That is why they spent hundreds of hours during the summer playing softball together. They needed to be part of a team. They wouldn't want to admit it, but they did need the love, support, and respect of other men.

FRIENDS

How about you? Do you sense a need for other men in your life? Do you have the kind of friends you want? How do you know they are your friends? What can you count on from these guys? What do you need more of from your friends?

Stop for a minute and ponder those questions. Jot down your insights. Then answer this question: Who can you call in the middle of the night to express your greatest fear and be assured that person will be there for you and support you? Write his name down right here. And list several reasons you know you can count on him. You'll appreciate him all the more when you see it in black and white.

My best guy friend is: Jim Hughes

How I know I can count on him: He's there to help me through this time of trial. He knows when someone's hunting.

Now let's talk more specifically about the importance of good male friendships.

A VITAL NEED

Every man has a deep need for meaningful, intimate relationships with other people, and specifically with other men. Paul says in 1 Thessalonians 2:7, "But we proved to be gentle among you, as a nursing mother tenderly cares for her own children." This quote touches on many aspects of a person's character, but note the word *we*. Paul, Timothy, and Silvanus came together to the Thessalonian church. They ministered together there. It is fascinating to see how often Paul uses the pronouns "we," "our," and "us."

Yet Paul was an individualistic, rugged, dynamic person. In 1 Corinthians 9:24–27 we read:

Do you not know that those who run in a race all run, but only one receives the prize? Run in such a way that you may win. And everyone who competes in the games exercises self-control in all things. They then do it to receive a perishable wreath, but we an imperishable. Therefore I run in such a way, as not without aim; I box in such a way, as not beating the air; but I buffet my body and make it my slave, lest possibly, after I have preached to others, I myself should be disqualified.

Notice here that Paul says, "I buffet my body and make it my slave." When I first began to study this text, I thought the word *buffet* meant one of those all-you-can-eat affairs you and I like to attend after church. I took this command seriously to "buffet my body." Imagine my shock when, as I studied the Greek, I realized it didn't mean to "pig out"! In fact, it means just the opposite.

Paul's concept comes from the ancient Greek practice of boxing with gloves made of rawhide strips embedded with bits of steel. The combatants would literally beat one another black and blue in the boxing arena. Paul wanted to bring every part of his life—his thoughts, his attitudes, his relationships, and his priorities—under deliberate subjection in order that he might win life's race.

In 2 Timothy 2, Paul again talks about the strenuous life we ought to live as Christians. He says in verses 3–6 and 9–10:

Suffer hardship with me, as a good soldier of Christ Jesus. No soldier in active service entangles himself in the affairs of everyday life, so that he may please the one who enlisted him as a soldier. And also if anyone competes as an athlete, he does not win the prize unless he competes according to the rules. The hard-working farmer ought to be the first to receive his share of the crops.

I suffer hardship even to imprisonment as a criminal; but the word of God is not imprisoned. For this reason I endure all things for the sake of those who are chosen, that they also may obtain the salvation which is in Christ Jesus and with it eternal glory.

We need others, but that need does not imply inherent weakness. Paul believed a man ought to be tough; he ought to pay the price; he ought to be committed; he ought to be rugged. And yet this same leader saw the vital need for interpersonal relationships. For example, he was very close to the elders of the churches he founded.

Paul was not the only one who saw a need for these relationships; the entire biblical record illustrates this principle. For example: David and Jonathan had a committed friendship; Moses shared a close relationship with Aaron; Jesus developed deep friendships with the apostles, particularly Peter, James, and John.

Time after time, the New Testament writers exhort us to act on our need for other people. We are not to attempt to stand alone.

The letter addressed to the Hebrews issues a warning call to unity, to brotherhood. Hebrews 3:12–13 instructs us:

> Take care, brethren, lest there should be in any one of you an evil, unbelieving heart, in falling away from the living God. But encourage one another day after day, as long as it is still called "Today," lest any one of you be hardened by the deceitfulness of sin.

THE NEED FOR BROTHERHOOD

Without the daily encouragement of other people, our natural tendency is to stagnate spiritually. This is one of the Bible's clear admonitions for Christians who feel that "God and I can make it alone." Scripture is clear in stating that we do need each other. In his first letter to the Corinthian church Paul says:

> And the eye cannot say to the hand, "I have no need of you"; or again the head to the feet, "I have no need of you." ... But God has so composed the body, giving more abundant honor to that member which lacked, that there should be no division in the body, but that the members should have the same care for one another. And if one member suffers, all the members suffer with it; if one member is honored, all the members rejoice with it. Now you are Christ's body, and individually members of it. (1 Corinthians 12:21, 24–27)

Do you get the point? God says we are all vital and we all need one another. That means you need me and I need you! It means you need other guys in your life. God doesn't want any of us to go it on our own.

Do you recognize this need in your own life? I mean, can you really believe that you need other guys and they need you?

As for believing others need me, I honestly don't have a problem with that. Please understand, I don't mean to sound self-absorbed here. But I have a public ministry and get to speak and write to many, many people every year. I receive letters, comments, phone calls, and other forms of feedback (even food!) demonstrating appreciation. I feel needed. I feel the same need from my family, friends, and coworkers.

But I do honestly struggle with needing others. There is a psychological test entitled the FIRO B that is used quite frequently by counselors. It helps point out how much a person desires to include or exclude people from his or her life. You get two scores—one for how much you want to include people and the other for how much you want others to include you. The scores range from 0 (extreme exclusion of people) to 10 (extreme inclusion of people).

I've taken the FIRO B several times and every time I come out about the same: 0–0. That is pathetic. It means my natural personality bent is to be an extreme loner. In other words, I don't want to have a party and I don't want to be invited to a party. I can travel all over the world, as I do routinely, and seldom experience loneliness. Me, myself, and I have a great time together!

Please don't get me wrong—I do love people, and I seek to act lovingly. I tend to be friendly, gregarious, and some even say likable. But I get empowered by being alone—not by being in a group. That isn't bad or good. It is simply the way I am (God had a lot to do with that).

However, I have learned over time, and am still constantly learning, that I do need people. I may not "feel" like it but the reality is, I do need friends.

I need your support as a friend. I need your insight. I need your backing. I need your love. I need your encouragement. I need your companionship. I need your time. I need your understanding. I need your gifts to complete me. I need perspective. I need you.

Knowing this, I have worked on building these kinds of friendships. I now have a few guys in my life with whom I enjoy deeper friendships. We are committed to one another, can call one another any time, can share our dreams and our fears and know we are understood and not judged.

One such friend is Ray. He and his wife Vicki and my wife Mary and I have all bonded. We vacation together; we spend time together on almost a weekly basis—meals, or shopping, or a movie. We all support one another, knowing that the others are there for us. Fundamentally, we know we are loved no matter what. Ray, who is also my pastor, said in a message the other day, "A friend is one who walks in the door when everyone else walks out." He is there when you need him—regardless of the circumstances. That is biblical brotherhood.

And in the process, we are becoming one. We are experiencing personal growth and a sense of real unity.

A PSYCHOLOGICAL NEED

While God's Word is the only source necessary to verify our need for relationships with other people, it's interesting that psychologists have also recognized this need. Harry Stack Sullivan, an eminent psychiatrist in the field of interpersonal relationships, has put forth the theory that "all personal damage and regression, as well as all personal healing and growth, come through our relationships with others. There is a persistent, if uninformed, suspicion in most of us that we can solve our own problems and be the masters of our ships of life. But the fact of the matter is that by ourselves we can only be consumed by our problems and suffer shipwreck."[1]

Further, in his book *Reality Therapy*, William Glasser contends that everyone has two great needs: (1) the need to be loved and completely accepted by someone, and (2) the need to love and accept someone else completely. Both of these needs have at their base the need for a meaningful, dynamic relationship.

LEVELS OF RELATIONSHIPS

Although it is obvious from the Scriptures that relationships are vital, it is also important to realize that we relate with people at different levels. There are four basic levels of relationship to keep in mind. I invite you to look at these types of relationships and identify which types you have with your particular friends.

First is the *concerned relationship*—a one-sided relationship that we initiate with everyone we meet. Here we have a responsibility to maintain a general spirit of love to all people.

The Living Bible pictures the type of love we are called to demonstrate:

Don't just pretend that you love others: really love them. Hate what is wrong. Stand on the side of the good. Love each other with brotherly affection and take delight in honoring each other. Never be lazy in your work, but serve the Lord enthusiastically.

Be glad for all God is planning for you. Be patient in trouble, and prayerful always. When God's children are in need, you be the one to help them out. And get into the habit of inviting guests home for dinner or, if they need lodging, for the night.

If someone mistreats you because you are a Christian, don't curse him; pray that God will bless him. When others are happy, be happy with them. If they are sad, share their sorrow. Work happily together. Don't try to act big. Don't try to get into the good graces of important people, but enjoy the company of ordinary folks. And don't think you know it all!

Never pay back evil for evil. Do things in such a way that everyone can see you are honest clear through. Don't quarrel with anyone. Be at peace with everyone, just as much as possible.

Dear friends, never avenge yourselves. Leave that to God, for he has said that he will repay those who deserve it. [Don't take the law into your own hands.] Instead, feed your enemy if he is hungry. If he is thirsty give him something to drink and you will be "heaping coals of fire on his head." In other words, he will feel ashamed of himself for what he has done to you. Don't let evil get the upper hand, but conquer evil by doing good. (Romans 12:9–21)

Many relationships will be of very short duration and possibly of fleeting import to us. We don't expect much from these relationships. In fact, they could be viewed as more or less casual; however, we should never be careless or unconcerned with them.

The second level to consider is the *corporate relationship*. God has placed each of us in specific areas of responsibility in our churches, our jobs, our civic activities, and our neighborhoods. In these, we have common goals and the relationship develops as we work together to get things accomplished for the good of a group or community. Whenever God places a person in close proximity to us in this way, we must again apply the principle of love portrayed in Romans 12:9–21.

The third level is the *committed relationship*. God wants us to establish this kind of relationship with a limited number of close friends or relatives who can hold us accountable, encourage us, and show us love in specific ways. This is sometimes found in small group settings in a church. These people are truly committed to one another, which ought to be the norm of any ministry group.

Please understand, you don't need to "feel" especially close to be committed—but you do need to be committed. One of the greatest disappointments I ever experienced was when I toured the U.S. and interviewed dozens of Christian leaders. Though the people in these church and parachurch ministries related well professionally, they lacked personal relationships. They lacked a spirit of unity and of honest caring for one another. This grieved me, and I believe it grieves the heart of God. We must be committed to those in our ministry groups if we are going to be effective for the kingdom.

The fourth level is the *covenant relationship*. This involves a deeper level of commitment between yourself and one or two other people. God places significant people in each life who greatly affect its course. Time and maturity serve to strengthen these covenants. The relationship with one's marriage partner is a prime example of the covenant relationship.

It is important, though, to have a close, covenant-level relationship with one or two other people as well—people with whom you can be utterly candid and from whom you will receive penetrating insight and honest advice for your own personal development.

"Brotherhood" is this deeper commitment to one another. It is manifested by relationships that go beyond the superficial and reflect honest, open caring and self-sacrifice.

In 1 Peter 2:17 we are told: "Honor all men; love the brotherhood, fear God, honor the king." God wants deeper, meaningful, powerful relationships for you and me. That is biblical brotherhood.

In the next chapter we'll look more closely at the principles of committed and covenant relationships, the kind that can develop into the team mindset we need.

For now, take a minute and evaluate your present relationships. List in the table below your five most significant men friends and identify which of the four types of relationship you presently have with each—casual (concerned), corporate, committed, or covenant. Then write what kind of relationship you would like to have with each.

NAME OF YOUR FRIEND	EXISTING TYPE OF RELATIONSHIP	DESIRED TYPE OF RELATIONSHIP
Jay Hughes	Corporate/Committed	Committed/Covenant
Matt Shriber	Committed	Committed/Covenant

Action Steps

Write the name of your closest friend below. Then list five things you can do to build into his life.

List five ways your friend ministers or could minister to you. What do you need?

CHAPTER THREE

BUILDING YOUR TEAM

Principles of a Team Relationship

So how are you feeling about the levels of relationships in your life right now? Are they strong enough, intimate enough, empowering enough? If you are like most of us, your answer will be something like: "Absolutely not. I need deeper and more meaningful relationships. I need a team."

Let's see what a real team, one based on truly committed relationships, looks like. Remember, if you don't have a strong team to work with, you'll never have the kind of impact God wants you to have in your family, church, community, or workplace. You need an infrastructure, a backup, a group of like-minded men committed to one another and going in the same direction. That spells *team*.

The team members in my business have a commitment-level relationship. Doug, Mary, Scott, the rest of the team, and I are all committed to one another, and this is powerful. We trust each other to be honest, diligent, loyal, and supportive.

When I think of developing this kind of commitment and covenant relationship in a team, my mind immediately goes to 1 Samuel 18–20 and the relationship David and Jonathan shared. Though they were only two men, their sense of belonging, commitment, and care for each other exemplified a true team mindset.

Jonathan, the son of Saul, became an intimate friend of David. We read that the soul of David was knit to the soul of Jonathan. Jonathan loved David as he loved himself, and the two became like brothers. That is the kind of relationship men need today—we need to be anchored firmly in a team of brothers.

Many principles can be gleaned from the allegiance between Jonathan and David. Let's survey a few of them as we study how to build commitment and covenant relationships. I encourage you to evaluate your own life and closest male friendships in light of these principles.

1. SELF-SACRIFICE

In 1 Samuel 18:4 we read, "And Jonathan stripped himself of the robe that was on him and gave it to David, with his armor, including his sword and his bow and his belt."

Jonathan became vulnerable when he let David have his means of protection and things that met his physical needs. Such vulnerability characterizes a special commitment to someone else: *I will deny myself for you and I will sacrifice for you.*

I often saw this wonderful spirit of self-sacrifice in the life of a former associate who worked with me for a while in Future Achievement International, a personal leadership company where I serve as chairman. Bill Smith had enjoyed a long and distinguished career in the navy. He'd graduated from the Naval Academy, received his master's degree, and rapidly moved through the ranks to become a captain. He succeeded in six major commands, including several ships. Eventually Bill became chief of staff for the Pacific Fleet Naval Command where, with a staff of 3000, he oversaw the training of 150,000 naval personnel around the world. Obviously, this guy was a seasoned pro.

Bill came to us to operate our new start-up organization, a highly entrepreneurial business. Most important, he came in with a servant spirit. Instead of demanding that everyone recognize his credentials and track record, Bill went to work. He committed to make a difference in the lives of guys like you and me, rolled up his sleeves, and started in. And every day I saw in him the qualities listed in the following chart.

How do you rate in these areas? Take a minute to examine the qualities Bill so vividly manifested, then rate your own servant attitude of self-sacrifice toward the members of your team (2 = weak; 10 = outstanding).

SERVANT QUALITY	BILL	ME
Seeking out needs to meet	10	2 4 6 8 10
Doing whatever it takes	10	2 4 6 8 10
Being teachable about own lack of experience in business	10	2 4 6 8 10
Encouraging everyone in the office	10	2 4 6 8 10
Working long and hard	10	2 4 6 8 10
Seeking no personal glory	10	2 4 6 8 10
Focusing on making others successful	10	2 4 6 8 10
Not demanding appreciation	10	2 4 6 8 10
Listening	10	2 4 6 8 10
Loving	10	2 4 6 8 10

2. Concern

"So Jonathan told David saying, 'Saul my father is seeking to put you to death. Now therefore, please be on guard in the morning, and stay in a secret place and hide yourself'" (1 Samuel 19:2).

Jonathan acted on his concern for David and sought to help him in every way he could. A committed relationship always involves practical demonstrations of concern for others on your team.

Paul teaches this in 1 Thessalonians 5:14. We are to "admonish the unruly, encourage the fainthearted, help the weak, be patient with all men." The point is to act on our commitment. Our concern should result in encouragement if any of our brothers are downhearted, help if they are going through difficulties, and admonition if they have room for improvement in any given areas.

One friend of mine always knows how to minister to me at the right time and in the right way. One day when I was particularly frustrated by a series of events, he came to me, put his arm around me, and said simply, "I love you, and I believe in you." He knew what I needed at that point. I didn't need someone to tell me I had a bad attitude and needed to change it. I needed someone to understand and demonstrate godly, committed concern.

My "Wake-up Calls"

On the other hand, at times I sin and do need to be admonished. Recently one of the men with whom I work came to my office and told me there was something in my life I needed to deal with in order to be the kind of man God wanted me to be. His words were difficult to accept because he touched a sore spot. However, he loved me enough to confront me. That is real concern—the kind of concern we need in today's male friendships.

In another instance, just a few months ago, I was conducting a conference on personal leadership. Some top business and ministry leaders from around the world were going through some of our Future Achievement leadership training. As I spoke of the importance of developing a mission statement, one of the Hawaiian leaders there questioned, "What is your mission statement?"

I responded, "To have the maximum impact on the maximum number of people for eternity."

This same brother came to me at the break and said, "Ron, I want to challenge you. You will never be able to accomplish your mission statement unless you adjust your eating habits. You will not live long enough."

Ouch! That hurt! It was hard to hear. But because this brother and I had an established friendship (this is very important—build a relationship first), I knew he was honestly concerned. And I knew he was absolutely right.

This wake-up call grabbed my attention. I evaluated what he said, directly began to learn about right eating habits, held a 40-day fast (20 days of water followed by 20 days of water, juices, and some soup), and went through an extensive internal cleansing process. This man's concern changed the course of my life. Amazing, isn't it? In the few months since his observation I now have established a new pattern for healthy eating.

That is the power of true biblical concern. We really care about someone and we act on it—not out of selfishness but out of selfless love.

How about you? Are you this concerned about your best friends? How could you enhance your level of genuine, selfless concern? What could you do to help develop this attitude among your team? Think and pray on these questions, then write your answers in the space below:

To enhance my level of selfless concern for friends:

To develop this attitude among my team:

3. VERBAL SUPPORT

"Then Jonathan spoke well of David to Saul his father" (1 Samuel 19:4).

Though King Saul was incredibly angry and wanted to kill David, Jonathan stood by his friend.

It's easy to undermine an individual by gossiping or by not speaking on his behalf when someone else criticizes. I not only need to speak highly of my friend; I also need to counter any negative remark by asserting my loyalty. In this same verse, Jonathan says to his father, "'Do not let the king sin against his servant David, since he has not sinned against you, and since his deeds have been very beneficial to you.'"

Can you see how assertively Jonathan supported David? Because he loved David, he spoke strongly and yet lovingly to his father about him.

One day as I talked with a friend of mine, he began to undermine another friend by criticizing some of his activities. I agreed that our friend had acted improperly, but then the speaker began to question the motives of the other person. I had to step in assertively and say, "Stop! I love you; I am committed to you; I do believe that this person has done something wrong and I will speak to him about it. However, you cannot speak negatively about his motives. Only God can question those, and I cannot let you speak about him that way."

When I did that, I risked the possibility of damaging my relationship with the friend who was speaking. However, because of a commitment to my other friend, I had to stand up for him.

Frankly, I find myself doing this almost every day. Because you and I carry so much sinful baggage with us, we tend to misunderstand others and not grant them the benefit of the doubt. Right? Just think of the last time a friend of yours spoke ill of someone else. While it's possible the other person did do something wrong, it's also possible he did not—the act may have been misunderstood. So what do you do if another friend brings up the problem?

A concerned friend stands in the gap, serving as peacemaker while lending perspective. You might say something like, "I understand your concern, but what about how he does———so well?" Or you might say, "Could you be misinterpreting the situation and not thinking the best?" These comments may help shine a new light on the situation.

You can also encourage direct communication: "You guys need to talk about this. I believe you have a point, but I believe———has one also. You each need to listen to the other person and work through this. I'll be glad to meet with you for clarification."

I pray that Christian men today will build concerned relationships in which we can have confidence that other men of integrity are standing up and supporting us as we do the same for them. Do you support your friend by verbally encouraging him in private and in public? By standing up for him, if necessary, among others? Such loyalty is critical to the building of a committed team.

4. OPENNESS

"Then David fled from Naioth in Ramah, and came and said to Jonathan, 'What have I done? What is my iniquity? And what is my sin before your father, that he is seeking my life?'" (1 Samuel 20:1).

Notice how transparent and open David was—he wanted to know what he had done wrong. And he was trusting Jonathan to level with him.

I believe he was honestly searching for an answer. One of the greatest needs in team relationships is such openness: the genuine willingness to admit a weakness and seek or share an answer. Communication must be aboveboard; nothing can be hidden. We must share with our closest friends what we are thinking and feeling about each other and about ourselves.

Some years ago, my wife and I and another couple spent seven months in a 20-foot motor home traveling around the United States. We covered 20,000 miles and thirty-seven states as we visited and studied 175 of the top churches in America. I was working on my doctorate, researching top Christian ministry leaders in America on leadership development—my lifelong passion.

Do you see this picture? Two couples, seven months, 20-foot motor home (we ate, slept, and traveled in it). We had one bed over the cab and another in the back where the kitchen table normally was. We hung up a thin sheet to separate "the holy place from the most holy place," as we liked to say.

Well, to say the trip was dynamic would be a classic understatement. It turned into one of the most profound experiences of our lives. God changed us all for the better. When we began, we were friends, but we didn't relate with one another naturally. In fact, my wife, Mary, and Theda, the wife of my friend, had little in common. Can you imagine two women with contrasting tastes, backgrounds, and interests living together in a motor home and sharing a six-square-foot kitchen area for seven months?

As we traveled, we started getting on each other's nerves. We had, however, made the commitment to love each other and to be encouraging, open, and honest. We learned quickly that openness and honesty are not the same as criticizing.

We learned, too, that honesty means sometimes sharing with others how we feel about areas of weakness in their lives.

One day we walked through a small town that had a fake saloon with a musical show inside. I happen to enjoy that kind of thing, and as we walked by I said, "Let's go in."

But they didn't want to. I said, "I really want to go!"

They laughed at me, poked some fun, and kept walking—not realizing that their rebuff actually hurt me a little. (I told you it was a very long trip!) I hung back and walked in silence.

Eventually Alan came back to me and asked, "Ron, are you pouting?"

"Yes," I admitted.

That silly incident turned into a healthy discussion of how each of us has a different perspective on things. No one blamed anyone else, but we began to discover how each of us felt, learning to see things from each other's perspective.

In fact, this led us to create a ranking system of 1 to 10. One meant you didn't care much one way or the other about an issue, and 10 meant it was vital to you. If one person wanted to do something at a 10 level, the others generally went along with him. When the ranking wasn't so high, we each were better able to identify how we felt about something and we could make more appropriate decisions together.

Although I didn't get my way in this particular situation, we all made progress in learning how to communicate our needs. Many times during the trip we evaluated our relationships with one another during dinner. The openness and honesty of those talks drew us together because of our commitment. All four of us agree that those months produced incredible spiritual growth in our lives.

How do you rank in your closest relationships regarding the issue of openness? Are you transparent and real, or do you disguise yourself? It's easy to project an image that doesn't line up with who we really are. I struggle with that and I imagine you do, too, since it's a common problem among even the most well-intentioned Christian men.

5. Availability

"Then Jonathan said to David, 'Whatever you say, I will do for you'" (1Samuel 20:4).

What an incredible statement of commitment! It says, "Whenever you need me, I will be there. I am willing to do whatever needs to be done whenever it needs to be done to help you."

I confess I find this particular quality difficult to maintain. I do not naturally want to be available to people—even to my closest friends. I tend to be oriented toward careful time management. My time is my territory and I can become upset when someone invades that territory. I want people to leave me alone when I am trying to keep to my busy schedule.

During the last few years, however, God has impressed upon me that He often moves with a sense of timing different from mine. I need to be sensitive to His Spirit when an opportunity to do something for someone, and thus for God Himself, arises. He has also shown me that if I am really committed to someone I will be willing to drop whatever I'm doing to help meet the needs of that person.

One day as I was working on this concept some years ago, my son came into my study. He wanted to show me what he had written that day. My little girl was waiting outside, needing to see me too. There I was, sequestering myself to study the issue of availability—while making myself unavailable to my own children!

God had provided a living illustration of what I needed to do. His message suddenly sank in. I left my study and gathered my family, kissed my son and hugged my wife. Then I bent down to kiss my two-year-old daughter, but she scratched me on the cheek and started to scream. Obviously, our being available doesn't necessarily mean we will always be rewarded. Self-sacrifice is sometimes a painful part of a covenant relationship!

My close friends will now hear me say, "If you ever need me anywhere, anytime, I'll be there." You see, they need to know I am their friend and they can count on me. Whether we've experienced failure or success, we need to connect with our friends.

6. AFFECTION

"When the lad was gone, David rose from the south side and fell on his face to the ground, and bowed three times. And they kissed each other and wept together, but David more" (1 Samuel 20:41). David and Jonathan loved each other. Oh, how we need to see that in team relationships today! People need to see our commitment to each other as Christian men so that non-Christians can say, "Oh, how they love one another!"

My wife and I had lunch recently with one of my dearest friends and his wife. We laughed; we shared; we ministered to one another, and we touched one another emotionally. It was obvious to us and to everyone around us that we had a deep affection for one another. We loved being together. I would do anything for that dear brother of mine, and I know he would do anything for me. That is the kind of enriching relationship we all need to share.

Now, stop and consider carefully the principles we've examined in this chapter. Our relationships need the qualities modeled by David and Jonathan in order for us to be strong and dynamic leaders in our homes, ministries, businesses and communities. We need the team!

Action Steps

Using the chart below, evaluate yourself in light of each of these principles. Identify where you are strong and where you are weak.

RELATIONSHIP PRINCIPLE	STRENGTHS	WEAKNESSES
Self-sacrifice		
Concern		
Verbal support		
Openness		
Availability		
Affection		

Determine one way you can bring more strength to your weakest attribute and write down how you will do it.

Write in the "Activity" space below one thing you can do this week to build a strong sense of team with your closest friends. Then write when and where you could implement your idea.

ACTIVITY	WHEN	WHERE

CHAPTER FOUR

Power in Control
Part One

A Disciplined Life

Some years ago, I was strolling through the Sears store near my former home in St. Davids, Pennsylvania, enjoying time with a particularly close friend. All of a sudden he turned, looked me in the eye, and right there in the Sears store he spat in my face!

Being a gentleman, I didn't say anything. I simply took out my handkerchief, wiped off my face, and continued walking.

After a few minutes, without any apology, he wryly looked at me and spat in my face a second time. I know you find this hard to believe, but it's absolutely true. Again I took out my handkerchief, wiped off my face, and continued to walk on. My friend didn't say a word.

Only a few more minutes later he looked at me, gave me this silly grin, and spat in my face one more time. Do you know what I did then? Nothing! Why? Because my friend was my six-month-old baby boy.

"Stupid," you say. Not really. Think about it! When you thought this true story involved two adults you were filled with repugnance and disbelief. After all, how could an adult treat someone else like that? All of us are mature enough to know we don't do that kind of thing (even if we sometimes feel like it). However, when I told you it was my baby son, you were not at all surprised. Infants are expected to act like infants.

Time to Put Off Childish Things

When we were children it made sense that we acted like children, but having become adults we are expected to act like adults. Yet I often see complaining and pouting and all kinds of childish behavior among adults, myself included.

Which brings us to a vital concept in our look at leadership: self-discipline. According to God's Word, it's a nonoptional attribute in the life of every Christian man:

> In pointing out these things to the brethren, you will be a good servant of Christ Jesus, constantly nourished on the words of the faith and of the sound doctrine which you have been following.... Discipline yourself for the purpose of godliness. (1 Timothy 4:6–7)

This goes along with 1 Corinthians 9:24–27, which we read in chapter 2. Our Lord commands and expects us to grow in personal discipline as a core quality of leadership at home, among friends, at work, or at church.

Quite frankly, I believe our society is in real trouble in this area. Our countries increasingly fail because our communities fail. Our communities fail because our institutions fail. Our institutions fail because our churches and ministries fail. Our churches fail because our families fail. Our families fail because we fail individually, as the leaders God appointed us to be.

I do a great deal of work among businesses, governments, and churches, and they all suffer from a lack of personal leadership. We rush out to learn new techniques, apply new programs, adopt new technologies, and embrace new management training programs. But all of these usually result in only short-term benefits. Why?

They don't work for long because individuals haven't changed.

All the government or business or church leadership programs in the world will not overcome this reality. We must start with ourselves. Good family management springs from good self-management. Good church management comes from good family management. Remember Paul's words to Timothy: "If anyone does not know how to manage his own family, how can he take care of God's church?" (1 Timothy 3:5, NIV).

Likewise, good business leadership is based on self-leadership. And good government is built on good self-government. It all comes back to self-discipline. To effectively take the lead among families, churches, institutions, communities, governments, and countries, it all starts with self-discipline.

With this mandate, let's examine (1) what self-discipline is, and (2) what we can do to grow in self-discipline.

WHAT IS SELF-DISCIPLINE?

The American Heritage Dictionary defines discipline as "training to produce a specified character or pattern of behavior, in moral or mental improvement."

In 1 Thessalonians 2 Paul relates that he, Timothy, and Silvanus proved to be a certain kind of people among the Thessalonians. In other words, Paul claims that their habitual lifestyle reflected certain kinds of positive activities and character: They acted as mature, steady individuals. They were models for the people of Thessalonica. These men were mighty, but their power was totally under the control of the Holy Spirit when they practiced self-discipline. They had "power in control."

How well do you function in the arena of self-control? To get an idea of your level of maturity in this area, evaluate yourself against the following examples of a godly, disciplined lifestyle by circling the appropriate number (1 = seldom practiced; 3 = practiced inconsistently; 5 = a consistent, formed habit).

Control of my tongue	1	3	5
Godly behavior	1	3	5
Spiritual leadership in the home	1	3	5
Practice of selfless love	1	3	5
Purity in thought and action	1	3	5
Daily quiet time (prayer and study of the Word)	1	3	5
Regular physical exercise	1	3	5

Your score should reveal whether you need to focus more specifically on the development of self-discipline. Most of us do! Over and over again, the apostle Paul talks about the need for self-control and its counterpart, self-sacrifice. A disciplined person may have to sacrifice time he had set aside for relaxation in order to complete an assigned responsibility. He is committed to hard work, but his work does not become workaholism or an excuse for playing the martyr. His self-discipline keeps his life in balance. And it helps him experience God's power and control.

Model a Positive Example

Discipline helps us model a positive example to those whom we lead. In 1 Timothy 4:12, Paul gives some instructions that I began to embrace some years ago when, at the age of twenty-nine, I became the president of a graduate school. I remember showing up at the campus the first week and some of the students asked me if I was a new student. I promptly answered, "Yes."

I was in far over my head. Who was I, a twenty-nine-year-old kid, to lead such a significant work? But these words of Paul gave me great comfort:

> Don't let anyone look down on you because you are young, but set an example for the believers in speech, in life, in love, in faith and in purity. (1 Timothy 4:12, NIV)

Notice that the issue is not age, but example. This told me I needed to start by being disciplined in the example I modeled to those around me.

Paul's admonition to Timothy spells out five areas in which you and I must model positive examples. (Use these questions to check yourself out.)

Speech

Do you control your tongue? Do you say those things that are good for edification, that meet the need of the moment as indicated in Ephesians 4:28–31? Do you build up or tear down?

Life

How is your conduct? What kind of behavior do you exhibit in public? in private?

Love

Do you practice the kind of love outlined in 1 Corinthians 13? Read that passage now and compare your own life to its teachings.

Faith

Are you a man of faith? Do you believe God for miracles? Do you trust in His sovereignty when things go wrong or when He doesn't answer in the way you would like?

Purity

How pure are you? Guys, lack of purity is a big problem today. Everywhere we turn, we face temptation (TV, movies, ads, and the overall sensuousness of our culture). How are you doing here? Do you rigorously practice what the following Scripture admonishes?

> Finally, brothers, whatever is true, whatever is noble, whatever is right, whatever is pure, whatever is lovely, whatever is admirable—if anything is excellent or praiseworthy—think about such things. (Philippians 4:8, NIV)

Think back over the last forty-eight hours of your life in light of that passage. How did you do? What do you need to work on in terms of personal purity before God and before others?

Pain, Focus, Perseverance

Let's be honest: The growth and exercise of self-discipline inevitably involves some pain. It also requires focus and perseverance.

Pain

Initially, there is nothing enjoyable about self-discipline; it can actually hurt!

As we saw earlier in 1 Corinthians 9, Paul said, "I buffet my body and make it my slave." Remember, the point of his illustration was that you and I must bring every part of our lives, including our bodies, into subjection through discipline that we may win the race of life and not be disqualified.

In one graphic moment, little Kerri Strug became a historic figure. You may remember her dramatic story. In the 1996 Olympic Games in Atlanta, the U.S. women's gymnastics squad was neck and neck with the competition for their first overall gold medal ever. The last event was the vault. Kerri missed her first vault, falling and severely injuring her leg. In obvious pain, she hobbled back to prepare for one final, determining vault. Then, to use the vernacular, she "sucked it up," sprinted down the runway, flew gracefully through the air and "stuck" her landing. She raised her hands signifying completion, then sank to the mat in agony. Her score in the vault won the gold medal for the U.S. women!

In just a few seconds, Kerri Strug provided a vivid illustration of how discipline might involve some pain. But it paid off—big time!

Focus

Building discipline also requires focus. We have to clearly identify what we want to change and then keep at it until our goal becomes reality.

Have you ever set a paper on fire with a magnifying glass? Because of the shape of the glass, the sun's rays concentrate on a focal point and, in time, the paper ignites. As you seek to grow in discipline, you are the magnifying glass, the rays of the sun are God's power, and the area of your life that needs changing is the paper. If you are determined to harness God's power and focus it on that area of your life, you will see change. But take away the magnifying glass—take away your willingness to change—and the paper will only gradually yellow in the sun's rays. The key is a willingness to focus your efforts on changing specific things in your life by harnessing the guiding power of God's Holy Spirit.

Perseverance

Growing in personal discipline requires perseverance on our part as we seek to develop new, better habits.

Have you ever made a commitment to grow in an area and then, after a period of time, become discouraged and quit? Me, too! Some of our best New Year's resolutions get broken before the fourth quarter of the Rose Bowl. Old habits die hard. To be conquered, they must be replaced with new ones.

Psychologists tell us it takes twenty-one consecutive days of right practice before something becomes a habit. So if you can establish a new behavior, stick with it and practice it consistently for twenty-one days, it will break the chain (at least initially) of the old habit and establish the new one. Perseverance is critical!

Once a new habit is well established through perseverance, you can move to begin changing another weak habit while reinforcing the new, healthy habit you've just established. Such perseverance is crucial to the growth of self-discipline.

Harness the Power of "Habit"

Wherever I consult or speak on how to grow in godly self-discipline, audiences have found the following acrostic to be extremely helpful:

> Have a plan.
> Allow God's power to work.
> Build an accountability structure.
> Internalize God's Word.
> Train consistently.

H: Have a Plan

Colossians 3 gives us the best strategy I've come across for growing personal discipline: *Put off the old man and put on the new man.* How's that for a simple and direct plan?

The way we begin to become disciplined is to eliminate those habits or inconsistencies that inhibit our walk with God. Just as a sanitation control manager (garbage collector) tosses off his smelly, rancid clothing and cleans up before he puts on his evening wear, so we must begin to grow discipline by tossing off the old man.

Putting on the new man refers back to replacing old bad habits with new good ones. It means we deliberately develop a new skill in place of the discarded one. We practice and practice and practice it until it becomes an integrated part of our life.

We'll continue our look at the HABIT acrostic in the next chapter. As we wrap up this chapter, I want to encourage you to pause and consider the quality of godly discipline you're experiencing in your life right now. Is this area of your life a strength or a weakness? Why or why not?

My friend, discipline, or "power in control," is the key to effective leadership in your home, among your friends, and in your church, business, or community. It may seem overwhelming, but don't worry. With the guidance and strengthening of the Holy Spirit, we can all grow in this pivotal area of life.

Action Steps

What did you learn as you scored yourself against the seven examples of a disciplined life? Write your answer here: *I am a failure at most of the examples —*

Look again at the five areas in which the apostle Paul admonished Timothy to provide a positive example. Circle the one you need to give the most attention to right now.

Speech   (Conduct)   Love   Faith   Purity

Write here the kind of circumstances that tempt you to be lax in this area: *Alcohol — Anger — Hurt others*

To launch your plan, articulate a positive new habit you can practice to replace the old habit. For example, you may wish to memorize Philippians 4:8 in order to fill your mind with pure thoughts. Then, whenever you are tempted to lust, you can meditate on that text. Write your new habit here: *Self Control*

Now write today's date and a statement in which you commit to "put off" the old habit daily for twenty-one days while "putting on" the corresponding new habit. *9/21/08 I will use (self-control) to change my habit of unrighteous conduct/Anger/critical words — Cursing*

Keep a daily log of your progress. Write down what is working and what isn't. Remember, press on toward twenty-one consistent days of practice. Enjoy the process as you look forward to your newfound "power in control."

At the end of the twenty-one days, evaluate your accomplishment. Do you want to follow the procedure again and attack another old, bad habit? Which one?

CHAPTER FIVE

Power in Control
Part Two

Growing in Discipline

A re you still with me? I guess so, or you wouldn't be reading this, right? Today let's take the concept of discipline a little further. You'll remember that we're using an acrostic to help us remember the key components:

Have a plan.
Allow God's power to work.
Build an accountability structure.
Internalize God's Word.
Train consistently.

In the last chapter we began the process by exploring the first component, "Have a plan." Now we will explore the other four elements of growth in self-discipline. It may encourage you to remember that, while it is difficult to put off a nasty old habit and put on a healthy new one, the beauty of new habits is that you don't have to think about them very much. Habits are built-in responses. Once they're established, you just do them! Godly men have developed godly habits that add up to godly self-discipline. Keep this in mind as we continue building positive new habits toward "power in control."

A: Allow God's Power to Work

The Scriptures say it is "not by might nor by power, but by My Spirit" (Zechariah 4:6) that God accomplishes His purposes. In other words, all our male might and power is for naught unless we yield ourselves completely to the power of the Holy Spirit, who is ready to work in and through us.

Nowhere is this more evident than in the story of the disciples on the day of Pentecost. Now remember, some of these men and women had turned against Jesus when He went to the cross. Judas turned Him in. Peter denied Him. Thomas doubted Him even after He rose from the grave. These guys acted like losers. They were overwhelmed, discouraged, frightened, and hopeless. But then something happened!

At Pentecost, God gave the Holy Spirit to these followers and, for the first time, they experienced the resurrection power of Christ. The same Peter who had cowered in fear and denied Jesus stood up before thousands on the day of Pentecost and boldly proclaimed the gospel. And God began to move.

The result? Thousands trusted Christ that very day. These disciples wholeheartedly gave their lives for the gospel and turned their world "right side up." They experienced real power—resurrection power. Not by their might nor by their power, but by the Holy Spirit.

But how do we let God empower us and, at the same time, be disciplined? In fact, often we're told to just stop trying and let God do it. That is good counsel. I remember some years ago a meeting with my boss, Dr. Bill Bright, president and founder of Campus Crusade for Christ. I was serving as president of that ministry's graduate school, the International School of Theology. I regularly met with Bill, who was not only a great boss but a close friend and associate. I also considered him my spiritual mentor.

"Divine" Wisdom

Bill was uncanny in his ability to say just enough to motivate me. On this particular day as I met with Bill in his office, I was struggling big time with the amount of money we had to raise for the school—tens of thousands of dollars weekly just to stay current. I was young (about thirty-three) and working as hard as I could. I would get up at 4 A.M. and go to a little hole-in-the-wall restaurant where I would pray (boy, would I pray), study the Word, and do my paperwork, so I could arrive at the office early and ready to hit the phones.

I approached Bill seeking "divine" wisdom. I remember the level of frustration I felt when his counsel to me was, "Ron, don't try so hard!"

"Don't try so hard? Don't try so hard? Are you kidding? I have bills to pay, payroll to meet, a faculty and student body to serve—and you say, 'Don't try so hard'? I thought I wasn't trying hard enough."

Bill just smiled and responded casually, in his peaceful manner. "Ron, it's not your battle to win; it's the Lord's. He will do it! Don't try so hard."

I am somewhat embarrassed to tell you that I didn't have the foggiest idea what he meant. And the fact that I didn't get it bugged me all the more. Out of pure frustration, I wrote off Bill's advice. I figured if I couldn't understand it, I couldn't apply it. And if I couldn't apply it, why try? Kind of sad, huh?

It is now sixteen years later, and only in the past year have I begun to grasp what Bill Bright meant that day in his office. His point was not that I shouldn't work hard or be disciplined. After all, he works anyone I know under the table, and he's in his midseventies.

Producing Fruit

Bill's point was that it is God's job, not ours, to produce the fruit in our lives; it is the "fruit of the Spirit" (Galatians 5:22). No matter how hard we try, we can't control or even manufacture that fruit. That was my problem. I was trying to finesse the fruit (money to run the school), to force the issue by sheer hard work. Bill's point was that I should stop trying so hard to control the outcome and instead trust God for the results. My responsibility was to continue to build into my life the roots of hard work and discipline, but to release my anxiety over results. In other words, I should focus on the roots and let God produce the fruit.

I've come to see that principle all the more clearly as Henry Blackaby has mentored me this past year through his lectures and his fantastic book, *Experiencing God*. Blackaby says, "Find out where God is moving and get on board."[1] Good advice! Historically, what I've done is get a "vision from God" and then pursue it with all my being (e.g., building the graduate school). Then, if I ran into a barrier, I would assume full responsibility and blast my way through by means of pure hard work.

In fact, I often quoted Robert Schuller's inspiring "Possibility Creed":

When faced with a mountain, I will not quit.
I will tunnel through it,
Climb over it,
March around it,
Or, if need be, turn that mountain into a gold mine.

Now, that's a great creed. But I took it to the extreme and unintentionally shoved God out of the equation. I simply stopped listening to the Lord, decreased my dependence, and increased my activity. And you know what? It just didn't work!

Now I am learning to handle that mountain differently. I continually ask the Lord, "What are You saying here? What are You doing? What do You want me to do? How should I proceed? Or do You just want me to wait?"

The results this year have been profound. In fact, it has been the most productive and significant year of my life. God has raised up more opportunities and led me into more strategic relationships and allowed me to see more lives changed than ever before. I have focused more on the roots (hard work, relational sensitivity, spiritual growth, discipline) and let God produce the fruit. And, wow! Has He produced fruit!

The key Scripture to remember in regard to the question of "your role versus God's role" is Philippians 2:12–13: "Work out your salvation with fear and trembling; for it is God who is at work in you, both to will and to work for His good pleasure."

It may help to look at it this way:

GOD'S ROLE	To give you the will (that gut desire) to do what you ought to do by means of the Word of God, the Holy Spirit, and other believers.
	To give you the power (that resurrection power of the Holy Spirit engendered by deep involvement in the Word) that enables you to tap into the living and mighty God.
YOUR ROLE	To "work out" your salvation (your growth in Christ personally and corporately) via discipline, commitment, obedience, and faithfulness.

So do your part. Work hard, build godly habits, and be disciplined in your obedience to God's call on your life. But let God be God; let Him do His part. If you harbor no unconfessed sin and truly seek His direction, He will give you the power and the right desires. He will work in and through you.

God will provide the right results, so don't sweat it, not even for a moment. Just keep cultivating those roots.

B: BUILD AN ACCOUNTABILITY STRUCTURE

When we know we should or shouldn't do something, why do we not just change? For instance, you know you should have a disciplined time with God every day. You know you should love your wife as Christ loves the church. You know you should practice routine physical exercise. But you don't diligently do it. Why not?

Though we may know something intellectually, we are not committed to it experientially. The bottom line is: We don't do what we know we should do because we simply don't want to. Period!

"What do you mean I don't want to?"

Admit it. You don't want to. You are not motivated to. It is not important enough to you for you to change.

So-o-o, you need to change your "want-to" factor. You can do this by creating simple accountability that prompts you to want to do what you know you ought to do.

Here is an accountability structure that I have seen work for thousands of men. Put it to work for yourself for one month. Faithfully practice this structure and watch your want-to factor soar.

Keep a "Dear Jesus" Journal

First, hold yourself accountable to God by journaling, keeping a private log. No one else needs to see it. By keeping it to yourself alone, you will be free to be more honest with God and with yourself.

Make it an ongoing "Dear Jesus" letter. *Recount* how you did yesterday in the area of discipline you are working on. *Respond* to what God tells you about any changes you need to make. *Refocus* your mind and heart on the issue at hand. And *recommit* to be the man God wants you to be.

Your daily log might look something like this:

Dear Jesus,

[Recount] Yesterday was about 6 on a 1–10 scale. I found myself tempted to lust 4 or 5 times through the day. I was able to "flee temptation" 3 of the 5 times but I found myself gazing at that ad in the newspaper and looking twice at a woman at the office.

[Respond] I confessed my sin immediately both times but found that the guilt lingered. I "hate" myself when I commit repeated sins. I need to accept Your forgiveness by faith. I also need to meditate on Colossians 3:1–17 at the moment of temptation.

[Refocus] Right now, I ask You to search me and see if there is any other sin in me. I long to be Your man and to be "pure in heart" so I can honor You and be used by You.

[Recommit] I submit my life to You today. By Your power I will "flee immorality" and "hunger and thirst after righteousness."

Remember, my brother, do this every day. Be honest, open, transparent. Share how you feel as well as what you did. The Lord will meet with you and you will sense clearly that you are walking "in the light" (1 John 1:7) because you are exposing your inner man to the light of truth. This personal accountability will start your new "reality check."

Give an Account of Yourself

Second, identify one or more trusted friends to serve as support men in your life, to hold you accountable. Together, you commit to openness, honesty, and trust as you open up your lives to each other. How? Once you have identified a group of guys and met a few times, ask for their help. You could say something like,

> Guys, I have learned that to be all God wants me to be I have to be accountable to Him. I try to do this daily in my times with Him, but I need a brother who will pray for me about specific areas and ask me tough questions. So, I would like to ask you to help me in that way. Right now one of the areas I am really working on is my *(thought life, abuse of my tongue, spiritual nurturing of my kids, etc.)*. My goal this week is to consistently *(apply Philippians 4:8, pray daily with my daughter, etc.)*. Please pray that I can do this and ask me next week how I did. And please be specific.

You could also agree on a set of written standards to which you will hold and encourage one another. A good source regarding the principles of discipline is 2 Timothy 2:3–6, 9–10, quoted in chapter 2 of this book. Also consider using the Promise Keepers organization's "Seven Promises of a Promise Keeper" as the basis for your mutual commitment to accountability:

> **A Promise Keeper** is committed to honoring Jesus Christ through worship, prayer, and obedience to God's Word in the power of the Holy Spirit.
> **A Promise Keeper** is committed to pursuing vital relationships with a few other men, understanding that he needs brothers to help him keep his promises.
> **A Promise Keeper** is committed to practicing spiritual, moral, ethical, and sexual purity.
> **A Promise Keeper** is committed to building strong marriages and families through love, protection, and biblical values.

A **Promise Keeper** is committed to supporting the mission of his church by honoring and praying for his pastor, and by actively giving his time and resources.

A **Promise Keeper** is committed to reaching beyond any racial and denominational barriers to demonstrate the power of biblical unity.

A **Promise Keeper** is committed to influencing his world, being obedient to the Great Commandment and the Great Commission.

The purpose of a devoted accountability team is to remind us of the seriousness of our commitments. It's much too easy to "slide by" in these areas of our lives. When brothers cover you in prayer and ask you tough questions (at your request), it drives home the fact that you must accept the responsibility of godly self-discipline.

This also creates a degree of potential discomfort when we sin. That's good! We need to feel more pain than pleasure over sin, and the accountability team will help.

Start a "Consequences Catalog"

The third and final accountability technique I recommend is a Consequences Catalog. Too often we simply don't discipline our lives because we don't anticipate the consequences of our actions. But what if you could look ahead five, ten, or forty years from now and see the consequences of today's attitude or behavior? What about seeing the *eternal* consequences of your behavior? Wow!

Paul said, "My ambition whether absent or present is to be pleasing to the Lord. For, we [Christians] shall all appear before the judgment seat of Christ [reward seat] that each one may give recompense for things done in the flesh, whether good or bad. Therefore, having the fear of God within me I admonish men" (2 Corinthians 5:9–11, from Jenson's Meditated & Amalgamated Version—what results when I have memorized Scriptures from several versions and they sort of run together in my mind. I thought I'd share this one with you. You're welcome.)

Paul was running scared! He feared the consequences of not living in a God-honoring way. And what are those consequences?

It's important to understand that Paul did not doubt his salvation unto eternal life. To try to be good enough to merit eternal life was not Paul's point. He knew that was a done deal, settled by grace through faith (Ephesians 2:8–9). But he also knew his actions did have consequences that included:

eternal rewards or the lack thereof, people who did or did not enter eternity because of him, the quality of his life on this earth, his personal usefulness, and so on.

To help you think into the future about probable consequences of your ongoing thoughts, attitudes, and actions, here's how to create and benefit from your own Consequences Catalog.

1. Choose an area of your life that needs better discipline (attitude, thought life, relationships, exercise, money management). Then briefly describe the situation as specifically as you can. (For example, anger toward your children leading to some type of verbal, emotional, or even physical abuse.)

2. Think of the possible negative consequences to your personal life (mental, emotional, physical, spiritual), your family, your friendships, your ministry, your work, your church, and your community if you do not "put off" this negative pattern and "put on" a positive new habit. Then briefly but specifically list those consequences. (For example: deeply crushing the spirit of a child, having a child never reach his or her full potential, hurting others because of a child's lack of growth, lacking closeness to a child, being emotionally distant from your wife, lacking usefulness spiritually, having a hardness of heart, grieving of the Holy Spirit.)

3. Think of the possible *positive consequences* of your developing the healthy discipline. Again, think of all critical areas of your life. Then list those positive consequences. (For example: honor to the Lord, personal usefulness spiritually, motivation of a child, closeness with your wife and children, a child's positive impact on others, a positive role model for others.)

Comparing lists 2 and 3 should strengthen your resolve and make it easier to be accountable.

I: INTERNALIZE GOD'S WORD

The fourth step in becoming disciplined focuses on the Word of God. Brother, you must let God's Word fill you consistently. Remember, we are transformed by the renewing of our minds (Romans 12:2). God changes us from the inside out by guiding us through new patterns of thinking.

Imagine a mountaintop. When the rains come they hit the mountain and then what happens? The water goes downhill. After time it develops into rivulets and then rivers. When more rains come and snow melts, the water flows into those rivers and escapes neatly down the mountain, sometimes ending up in an ocean.

This often happens with a behavior as well. It starts in our life as rain (a thought), which ultimately turns into a river (a habit). One author explains it this way:

> Sow a thought; reap an act.
> Sow an act; reap a habit.
> Sow a habit; reap a character.
> Sow a character; reap a destiny.

The key is to get the right thoughts into your mind and keep the wrong thoughts out, and one of the best ways to accomplish this is to focus on a Scripture over and over again until it becomes a part of you. Joshua 1:8 (NIV) says,

> Do not let this Book of the Law depart from your mouth; meditate on it day and night, so that you may be careful to do everything written in it. Then you will be prosperous and successful.

Meditate on it day and night. How do you meditate? Let me share a method that I've really enjoyed in recent years. You choose a passage of Scripture dealing with the area where you want to become disciplined, then apply what we might call the "3M" formula.

1. *Memorize it!* Yes, I said memorize it. You must be able to recall it at any point of temptation.

2. *Mull it over in your mind!* Picture what it says and chew on it as a cow chews on her cud. Keep thinking about what the words mean, how you need to apply it, and what the consequences will be if you do or don't apply it.

3. *Mind it!* Be obedient. Do what it says.

Let's imagine you are dealing with worry and feel the need to develop a new habit of trusting the Lord. The passage below is one of the all-time biblical classics on finding peace in the midst of turmoil. Read it right now and practice the "3Ms" (memorize, mull over, mind).

> Do not be anxious about anything, but in everything, by prayer and petition, with thanksgiving, present your requests to God. And the

peace of God, which transcends all understanding, will guard your hearts and your minds in Christ Jesus (Philippians 4:6–7, NIV).

You're well on your way!

T: TRAIN CONSISTENTLY

This final step in developing a disciplined lifestyle is where the rubber meets the road. Here is where patterns are built into your life. How do you train? You practice, practice, practice! For the next twenty-one days I challenge you to take seriously the action steps that follow. When you do, you'll begin to realize the true freedom that comes through discipline and gain a much greater sense of "power in control."

ACTION STEPS

This time our action steps are prepared to get you started on what we have discussed in the last two chapters.

Have a plan. Identify an area needing discipline. Write down the bad habit and a positive replacement (e.g., put off impure thoughts and put on pure thoughts, or put off worry and put on trust).

Allow God's power to work. Let God continue to give you the right desires and insights through prayer and His Word. Appropriate His power (e.g., say, "I am needy, and I depend on Your resurrection power to stay pure.").

Build an accountability structure. Write your "Dear Jesus" letter every day. Have at least one trustworthy Christian guy hold your feet to the fire (asking tough questions) often. Record and contemplate the consequences of developing or not developing your new habit.

Internalize God's Word. Memorize a key passage and meditate on it at least four times each day (early a.m., lunch, dinner, later p.m.). Jump to that passage each time you are tempted (e.g., Colossians 3:5–8 for lust, or Philippians 4:6–7 for worry) and mind what it tells you.

Train consistently. Practice the HABIT acrostic with this new discipline for twenty-one days, and rejoice in the results. Then select a new discipline you want to bring into your life and repeat the process!

CHAPTER SIX

GENTLE, NOT TIMID

The Incredible Power of Gentleness

Two men enter their homes. Each finds that his son has conducted an experiment in the living room with the chemistry set he was given for his birthday. The experiment explodes, and the chemicals leave a large hole in the new carpet and small holes in most of the furniture. Each son had been told that experiments are to be conducted only under the supervision of an adult and only in the garage. How does each dad react?

The first dad, Dave, explodes with a force greater than the chemistry explosion. He threatens to ground his son for twelve years and make him use his college savings to pay for the damage. Of course he realizes his threats are preposterous and he will never carry them out. *This is being a man,* he reasons. *First, show your strength, but then back off and be gentle, too.*

The second dad, Roger, nearly faints when he sees the damage, but rather than getting angry he feels that "boys will be boys" and that his job as a father is to encourage his son's creative genius. He hurries to have the damage repaired before his wife returns from visiting her mother.

Which father's reaction was right? Which reaction might be most akin to your own?

I maintain that neither was right. Each reaction was extreme, and each had both good and bad elements. The first dad, while obviously concerned about his son's feelings, was not consistent and not legitimately gentle. The second did not want to upset his wife and acted as peacemaker so as to avoid an unpleasant scene. However, he was not decisive—he displayed weakness, and that was not legitimately gentle.

The ideal model of an attitude for that kind of situation is typified by Paul. In 1 Thessalonians 2:7, Paul says he was "gentle among you, as a nursing mother tenderly cares for her own children." Do you understand the significance of the comparison? Paul says we are to be, in attitude and action, like that nursing mother. The key word in the passage is "gentle."

This chapter will deal with the concept of gentleness. One writer has said that gentleness is not a rippling little brook bubbling through the meadow; rather, it is the mighty ocean softly kissing the sands of the shore.

Yet gentleness is a quality often misunderstood among men. Unfortunately, many of us tend to think of it as unmanly, as wimpish. After all, how can we exude masculinity if we are to be like nursing mothers? So let's begin by exploding some widely held myths regarding gentleness and then develop some of its specific positive qualities. I think we'll see that true gentleness is incredibly powerful.

WHAT GENTLENESS IS NOT

When you hear the word "gentleness," what comes to mind? Do you think of a weak, passive, overly emotional, indecisive individual? Or do you think of a caring, involved, assertive, and sensitive person? Although I think of the latter, I believe some of us may have developed a few misconceptions about gentleness. Let me suggest in this section what gentleness is *not*.

Gentleness Is Not Weakness

To better understand this and the other things which are not true of gentleness, let's look at 1 Thessalonians 2:1–6.

> For you yourselves know, brethren, that our coming to you was not in vain, but after we had already suffered and been mistreated in Philippi, as you know, we had the boldness in our God to speak to you the gospel of God amid much opposition. For our exhortation does not come from error or impurity or by way of deceit; but just as we have been approved by God to be entrusted with the gospel, so we speak, not as pleasing men but God, who examines our hearts. For we never came with flattering speech, as you know, nor with a pretext for greed—God is witness—nor did we seek glory from men, either from you or from others, even though as apostles of Christ we might have asserted our authority.

In verse 7 Paul writes, "But we proved to be gentle among you." Note the word "but." Paul says in effect, "In contrast to how we could have lived, we have lived gently." We see the contrast particularly in verse 6 where he says they could have asserted themselves rightfully as apostles but didn't.

Notice in verse 2 that Paul clearly makes the point that gentleness is not weakness. He, along with Silvanus and Timothy, had been mistreated on many occasions. They had gone through tremendous opposition and pain. But as good soldiers they had persevered. They were tough.

In Acts 16:22 and following, we get a clearer idea of how Paul had been treated. Luke reports that the chief magistrates

> tore their robes off them and proceeded to order them to be beaten with rods. And when they had inflicted many blows upon them, they threw them into prison, commanding the jailer to guard them securely; and he, having received such a command, threw them into the inner prison, and fastened their feet in the stocks. (Acts 16:22–24)

Here were the great apostle Paul and Silas, a godly man of tremendous authority, being treated shamefully. But Paul sums up his attitude toward this type of treatment as he writes to the Corinthians:

> But we have this treasure in earthen vessels, that the surpassing great-ness of the power may be of God and not from ourselves; we are afflicted in every way, but not crushed; perplexed, but not despairing; persecuted, but not forsaken; struck down, but not destroyed; always carrying about in the body the dying of Jesus, that the life of Jesus also may be manifested in our body. For we who live are constantly being delivered over to death for Jesus' sake, that the life of Jesus also may be manifested in our mortal flesh. So death works in us, but life in you. (2 Corinthians 4:7–12)

Paul makes an important point here. When he says they were gentle, he isn't talking about weakness or timidity. These were men of incredible fortitude and commitment. Gentleness and strength are not mutually exclusive traits.

Gentleness Is Not Ineffectiveness

Paul says in 1 Thessalonians 2:1, "For you yourselves know, brethren, that our coming to you was not in vain." The words "in vain" here can be translated "fruit-less." Paul says, "We were not fruitless—we were fruitful. We were productive."

The synergy of these three men working together made their team particu-larly powerful; they clearly had a significant impact upon the people. Their ministry was fruitful and effective. In 1 Thessalonians 1, we see that because of Paul, Timothy, and Silvanus's ministry, the Thessalonian believers became examples to all the believers in Macedonia and in Achaia.

Gentleness Is Not Lack of Confidence

Paul points out in 1 Thessalonians 2:2 that "we had the boldness in our God to speak to you the gospel of God amid much opposition." There is no timidity in this statement. They were bold; they were open and direct and assertive; they spoke despite the opposition they faced. They didn't hold back even when the message caused conflict.

It has been tough for me to be strong when I receive opposition. I've realized over the last few years that I need to be liked. I don't like people not to like me.

I learned an important lesson about this when I was in college. I had just begun to communicate my faith in Jesus Christ with people. In my opinion, I shared my faith lovingly and warmly, but assertively. But then a friend from another Christian organization came to me and said I was being offensive and pushy. As a result, I became highly introspective and for four or five months I stopped sharing my faith entirely.

Then God made it clear to me that He wanted me to please Him, not people, and that if my goal in life was to be liked by people, I would never be satisfied and would never be a strong man of God. I reviewed the advice of my friend and did try to be more sensitive as I depended on God to work in me and through me. I became bold even in the face of some tremendous opposition. I don't know if people really like me now, but I don't seem to have many enemies, and for that I am grateful! I've found that boldness tempered with true gentleness goes a long way in practically any area of life.

Paul goes on to say that he and his companions were bold not only in the midst of opposition but also were bold "in our God" (verse 2). Their boldness was not simply a natural courage; it was inspired by God. They sensed that God had called them to speak. Likewise, we need to be confident and assertive in dealing with negative issues in the lives of people whether at work or at home, because God has placed us in responsible positions and wants us to speak with authority. This presupposes, of course, that we have an intimate relationship with God.

Gentleness Is Not Flattery

Paul says in 1 Thessalonians 2:5–6, "We never came with flattering speech, as you know, nor with pretext for greed—God is our witness—nor did we seek glory from men, either from you or from others." Paul was not afraid of offending people by pointing out areas in their lives that needed improvement. Sometimes he unsettled their complacency by pointing out their weaknesses.

Paul, Timothy, and Silvanus also realized that God was examining their hearts. They knew they were to be God-pleasers and not people-pleasers. Therefore, they were direct. They encouraged and affirmed others, but they also pointed out sin and failings when necessary. They consistently did what would glorify God and meet the spiritual needs of the people.

Like Paul's team, we can be gentle yet direct when we point out problems. This may hurt the other person momentarily, but if done in love it can result in his or her spiritual growth and glory to our Lord.

Gentleness Is Not Passiveness

Look again at 1 Thessalonians 2:2–6 and note the action words. Paul says they were mistreated, they were bold, they spoke, they exhorted, they came, they sought. Paul, Timothy, and Silvanus were anything but passive. They were totally involved in the lives of other people.

Neither are we to be passive when we encounter sin, for fear of "offending" someone or some special interest group. Scripture makes a case for proper anger:

> And He made a scourge of cords, and drove them all out of the temple, with the sheep and the oxen; and He poured out the coins of the moneychangers, and overturned their tables; and to those who were selling the doves He said, "Take these things away; stop making My Father's house a house of merchandise." His disciples remembered that it was written, "Zeal for Thy house will consume Me". (John 2:15–17)

Righteous wrath is noble. It is demanded in Scripture if a man is to be strong in God's image. It was Jesus' particular love for the man with the withered hand that created within Him a tremendous anger against those who were denying that man his healing (Mark 3:5). It was Jesus' love for His Father that created His anger against the mercenaries who had degraded the house of worship and made it a "den of robbers" (Matthew 21:13). As leaders we, too, must be angry at the injustice, abuses, and sins that dishonor God and harm and enslave people.

Gentleness Is Not Indecision

One of the great qualities of any leader is decisiveness. He must have the confidence to make right decisions. Paul, Timothy, and Silvanus decisively addressed these people of Thessalonica. They knew their exhortation did not come from error or impurity or by way of deceit. They knew their motives were pure. They knew their methods were sound and their message true. They could be completely and undeniably honest because they were seeking to please God and because they knew they could hide nothing from God.

Someone has said that personality is what men see and character is what God sees. Put another way, personality is what I am in public and character is what I am in private. Scripture clearly reveals that these men were the same in private as they were in public. They acted both publicly and privately with absolute openness; they knew God had commissioned them and they knew they were speaking God's Word.

We need men today with that kind of openness in motive, method, and message. Our country, indeed our world, is looking for men of direction who know they are speaking God's words. Our marriages and our families need men who make decisions based on an absolute standard of right and wrong.

Think of the Iran Contra hearings, Koreagate, Whitewater, White House fund-raisers, and other local, state, and federal scandals of the last several years. All of these have roots in someone's lack of moral decisiveness. Men made poor decisions because they ignored moral standards. Men denied right decisions because they ignored moral commitment. And men used other people as scapegoats because they ignored moral responsibility.

This state of affairs must change if our country is to change. We must find men who are willing to accept full responsibility for failure or success, who make wise decisions based on God's absolute standards of right and wrong.

What Gentleness Is

How have *you* perceived gentleness during the course of your life? Have you thought of it as unmanly, ineffective, weak, or any of the other stereotypes we've just surveyed? If so, I heartily encourage you to begin to understand gentleness for what it actually is: a desperately needed core competency for personal leadership in your home, church, and business. If you can consistently practice the art of true gentleness, you will have an awesome impact on those around you.

I have gone to great lengths to explain what gentleness is not in order to dispel the myth that gentleness is the antithesis of masculinity. Now let's look more closely at what gentleness is—gentleness as God intends it, as His Son modeled it, and as Paul, Timothy, and Silvanus lived it.

You may recall Paul's metaphor: "We proved to be gentle among you, as a nursing mother tenderly cares for her own children" (1 Thessalonians 2:7). Now that we're secure in the fact that gentleness is fully compatible with masculinity, let's use Paul's metaphor to see how gentleness plays out in real life. What will you and I "look like" if we are being gentle in the fullest sense of the word?

I often watched as my wife, Mary, nursed our two children. As I think on Paul's metaphor of the nursing mother tenderly caring for her child, I realize I've observed at least four special qualities in a nursing mother, qualities that were also present in the lives of Paul and his teammates.

Gentleness Is Identifying and Meeting Needs

When a mother tenderly cares for her child, she looks out for his every need. Obviously the greatest need a baby has is for food. Whenever that little one is hungry, he cries. He is simply expressing his need.

When Paul talks about a nursing mother tenderly caring for her child, he pictures a prompt, loving response to someone's need. The words "tenderly cares" are translated in one Bible version as "cherishes." This term is also found in Ephesians 5:28–29, where Paul exhorts husbands to love their wives as they love themselves. He amplifies this by saying, "For no one ever hated his own flesh, but nourishes and cherishes it." His point is that we do cherish ourselves, specifically our flesh, and we should similarly cherish our wives.

If I injure myself by hammering my hand rather than a nail, I will not slap my hand or starve myself that day because I am mad at my hand for hurting. Rather, I will care for my hand, bandage and protect it, and pay extra attention to all my other personal needs as well. That kind of care is what Paul means here. We are to be gentle toward other people by cherishing them, by taking initiative to help meet their particular needs.

This kind of caring requires tremendous empathy, and the result is what Charles A. Parkhurst describes as "two hearts tugging on one load." Often people make no distinction between sympathy and empathy, but there is a vast difference. Sympathy is when I see someone hit his thumb with a hammer and I say, "Oh, that's too bad." Empathy is when that same person hits his thumb and I say, "Ouch!" Empathy is feeling *with* someone whereas sympathy is simply feeling *for* someone.

When my son Matt was five, he had a very tenderhearted friend named Brooke. One day when they were playing together, Matt got a terrible sunburn. Ugly blisters covered his little red shoulders. As my wife changed his shirt and Matt whimpered because of the pain, Brooke wound up all the anger he could muster and said, "Matt, if the sun ever does that to you again, I'll hate it!" That is empathy—Brooke felt the pain with Matt and hurt because his friend hurt.

How about you? Do your family members, teammates, and friends sense such empathy from you? Do they really know you understand how they feel about things? Do they sense that you truly "feel with them"? Gentleness identifies and meets needs.

Gentleness Is Being Tender

As I watched Mary nurse our little boy and later our little girl, the tenderness she showed and the warmth of those moments deeply impressed me. *Vincent's Word Studies* notes that the word "cherish" or "tenderly care" comes from the root word "warm." When you cherish someone, you are warm toward him. As a mother holds her child in her arms and softly strokes his little body with her hands and plays with his little fingers and kisses the top of that fuzzy little head, she exemplifies the tenderness and warmth God wants His people to share with others.

Tenderness comes more easily to men when we remember that every person is made in the image of God. Everyone, therefore, needs and deserves to be handled with the utmost sensitivity. I recoil at such popular book titles as *Creative Aggression, Winning through Deception and Selfishness,* and *Winning through Intimidation.* Of course we need to be direct, honest, and even forceful at times. But the kind of mentality espoused by these books is callous, calculating, and insensitive to the great worth of each individual. It is in no way acceptable. It is in no way tender.

I wish I could put a big sign on everyone I know that says, *HANDLE WITH CARE!* No matter how tough we think we are, we all need that kind of handling.

Unfortunately, I can be an insensitive clod, and I'm afraid I sometimes blow it when it comes to handling others with care.

Here's what happens. Someone in my office doesn't perform to my specifications (I have pretty high expectations for myself and for others). I get frustrated and angry internally. Then I make a veiled but noticeably hard comment. Ouch!

Now understand, the fact that I am dissatisfied or even angry may not be the problem. Dissatisfaction, even anger, can be a great motivator to correct real wrongs. The problem is how I deal with the issue. Instead of thinking through or praying about the needs of the person, I inappropriately express my anger. I don't shout or get nasty but I do become forceful and, too often, offensive. As the leader of my company, it's important that I deal with the performance issue—but I need to do so *gently.*

If I respond in anger or with an insensitive remark, what happens? I hurt a very good person whom I love dearly. I harm the relationship. I dishonor God with my lack of tenderness.

I inadvertently did this just a few days ago when I came down on a brother over the phone. I didn't think I was too harsh, but apparently I grieved him and damaged our relationship. I now have the responsibility—and the joy—of asking forgiveness for how I communicated. Again, it is not *what* was at issue, it was *how* it was addressed.

Of course you never have this problem, do you? Or are you a member of the Insensitive Clod Society like me? Let's covenant together to become tender "like a nursing mother." And, hey, that means being patient, too. That's next.

Gentleness Is Patient

When Mary was breast-feeding our infant son, she demonstrated the most incredible calmness with him. Whether he screamed out for food (many times) in the middle of the night or clamped down to take a big bite of her, she took it all in stride, knowing it was part of the nurturing process.

Now that's patience!

An epidemic of influenza broke out in a one-doctor town. The physician had had very little sleep for a week when he called on a patient with pneumonia. "Begin counting," he directed as he leaned over to hear the patient's respiration.

The doctor was so fatigued that he fell asleep with his head on the sick man's chest. It seemed but a moment when he awoke suddenly to hear the patient saying, "10,888; 10,889…"

That's patience!

I heard a man share the other day about his request to an airline ticket agent. He said, "I would like you to send this piece of luggage to Dallas, this piece to Anchorage, this one to Manila, and this one to Bangor, Maine. And I would like to go to Chicago."

The ticketer responded, "I can't do that!"

The traveler calmly replied, "Sure you can—you did it last week!"

When things don't go the way we like, we need this kind of patience!

The hardest place to have patience seems to be in our personal relationships. Even the apostle Paul, great as he was, lost his patience in dealing with John Mark (see Acts 15:36–40). Hudson Taylor once made the confession, "My greatest temptation is to lose my temper over the slackness and inefficiency so disappointing in those on whom I depend. It is no use to lose my temper…it is such a trial."

Having patience becomes particularly difficult when we have to deal with the ineptitude of other people. Here is where we need balance, since we also have a responsibility to point out weaknesses when they exist. We saw in the first part of 1 Thessalonians 2 that Paul, Timothy, and Silvanus would clearly point out sin when necessary.

However, we must be particularly patient as we point out weaknesses. Romans 15:1 (NIV) guides us: "We who are strong ought to bear with the failings of the weak." One evidence of maturity in male leadership is a willingness to "adapt our stride to the slower pace of our weak brother, while not forfeiting our lead. If we run too far ahead, we lose our power to influence."[1]

Have you ever found yourself in a discussion with someone who begins to go down all sorts of bunny trails in the conversation? You know, someone who talks about all sorts of issues and you don't have a clue as to where he or she is heading. Impatiently, you might say, "Just give me the bottom line."

Let me share a tip here. It may be that, like me, you manifest a lack of patience when a certain internal button is pushed. A button can be any circumstance that "hacks you off"—a whining child, a "nagging" wife, a bad day at work, a brother who doesn't follow through on a commitment, or a friend who talks in bunny trails.

Take a minute and make an honest list of your buttons. Then mentally practice how you *should* respond versus how you *do* respond. If you, through repetition, can turn a gentle, patient response into a habit, you will make great advances in this area.

Gentleness Is Giving Time

My wife spent untold hours with our infants feeding them and caring for them. She responded to their needs around the clock and willingly gave of her time. I know of no greater way to see gentleness in action than to see someone give so willingly of her time.

There is perhaps no greater gift. Once an hour is spent, it can never return. Everyone knows time is precious. A gentle man knows enough not to spend it all on himself.

Are you a gentle man? God says gentleness is to be an integral part of a man's total character. It isn't optional for us. We must, therefore, exercise the strength it takes to be gentle in every circumstance. And in the process we'll make a wonderful discovery: the incredible power of gentleness.

Action Steps

This week, identify one person with whom you need to be more gentle. Then develop a strategy to do just that. Be sure to incorporate a specific application of the four elements of gentleness: meeting needs, being tender, demonstrating patience, and giving time.

My Buttons:
finger pointing —
blaming —
Tonalities —
critical —
passive agressive comments —

CHAPTER SEVEN

The Power of Affection
Part One

Developing Intense Christian Love

D o you have a secret obsession? Something you continually crave? Something you can't get out of your mind? I have. Bakery goods! I love donuts. There used to be a place called the Dough Nuttery near my home in Philadelphia. Whenever I would get within a mile of the Dough Nuttery, visions of one of their special hot cinnamon rolls would flash through my mind. I could see the steam coming off the top and the butter melting down the sides. I could smell it; I could feel it; I could taste it. I would start to salivate. I just couldn't get that cinnamon roll out of my mind.

Now, donuts aren't nearly as important as people; but sometimes I find it easier to love my cinnamon roll than to love my fellow Christian. And yet Christians are supposed to have a deep affection, an intense love, for one another. Paul says in 1 Thessalonians 2:8 (KJV), "So being affectionately desirous of you, we were willing to have imparted unto you, not the gospel of God only, but also our own souls, because ye were dear unto us." Can you sense the intensity of feeling Paul had for these people?

According to the *Theological Dictionary of the New Testament,* Bible scholars believe the phrase "affectionately desirous," which occurs only this once in all of the New Testament, means a "warm, inward attachment" or "to feel oneself drawn to something or someone with intense longing." (Sounds like my thoughts toward cinnamon rolls.) The words translated "very dear" (in the NASB) are found several times throughout the New Testament and are even more often translated "dearly beloved." Paul says that he, Timothy, and Silvanus not only had a fond affection for these people, but that their ministry flowed out of that great love.

This concept of a significantly emotional attachment to other people runs throughout all of Scripture. All we need to do is look at such passages as Genesis 45:14–15; 1 Samuel 16:1 and 20:41; Luke 7:38–39; Acts 20:37–38; and Romans 16:16 to see the intensity of the genuine affection God's people shared in Bible times.

This same intensity must be true of our love for one another if we are to call ourselves strong Christian men. We are not only to be assertive, bold, and mighty, but within that strength we also are to be gentle, affectionate, and caring at the deepest level of our being. We are not only to be logical, bright, intelligent, and astute, but we also are to be sensitive, compassionate, and free to express real emotion.

Most of us have at some time pulled away from people, closing ourselves off from intimacy or vulnerability. But we can't ultimately be happy that way; neither can we experience Christian maturing or fulfillment. Instead, we need to enjoy a wholehearted affection for others.

How do you rate in this area? Are you more tough or more tender? Do you feel affection? Do you demonstrate it? Have you recognized its power? What would your wife say? What would your brothers in Christ say? Keep that in mind as we press on through this chapter. If you can "get this" and make it work, it will revolutionize your relationships—across the board!

It's important for us to realize that the fond affection Paul writes about does not just happen. It is a blessing God gives when we commit ourselves to one another. In this and in the next chapter we will look at six different ways in which God can help us develop a genuinely fond affection for the people around us. We can cultivate this kind of invigorating Christian love by taking six proactive, continuous steps in our relationships in harmony with the Holy Spirit's guidance and power. As you read the list below, you will note one key word that is common to all six steps.

SIX STEPS TOWARD FOND AFFECTION

1. Feel Positive Emotions

2. Think Positive Thoughts

3. Focus on the Positive in People

4. Offer Positive Prayers

5. Speak Positive Words

6. Practice Positive Actions

1. FEELING POSITIVE EMOTIONS

We can never have a binding friendship with someone unless we experience honest affection for him. Such attraction may come naturally if the two of you already have something in common. But what if the person you know you should love is hard to get along with? What if he is just "not your type"?

One of the easiest ways to abort affection for someone is to entertain negative emotions like anger, unforgiveness, suspicion or lack of trust, or bitterness. Such feelings must be conquered if we are to lead successful Christian lives: "But now you also, put them all aside: anger, wrath, malice, slander, and abusive speech from your mouth" (Colossians 3:8). Later in Colossians we are instructed:

> As those who have been chosen of God, holy and beloved, put on a heart of compassion, kindness, humility, gentleness and patience; bearing with one another, and forgiving each other, whoever has a complaint against anyone; just as the Lord forgave you, so also should you. (Colossians 3:12–13)

You'll recall from an earlier discussion that Paul says we can "put off" and "put on" emotions almost like a set of clothes. Imagine you are a garbage man. You have worked with the smelly stuff all day. When you come home, you need to get ready for a coat-and-tie dinner, so you put on your fanciest clothing right over your filthy work clothes. Ridiculous? You're right! But no more so than trying to "put on" Christian love over "filthy" anger and bitterness.

If we try to put on love, gentleness, and compassion without throwing off our dirty clothing of anger, wrath, and lack of forgiveness, there is no way we can really love someone. We can try to put on good qualities before we put off the bad ones, but those efforts are destined to fail because the old smelly clothes will invariably reek through. We must first put off the old by confessing and turning from our sin, asking God to give us the victory over negative attitudes. Only then can we put on the new and begin to experience the power of genuine Christian love.

Forgiveness Is Crucial

Without experiencing and extending forgiveness in our relationships, we will stay absolutely immobilized. Think about what bitterness did to Leonardo da Vinci.

One of the great intellects of his day, da Vinci was known for many accomplishments, including his masterpiece, *The Last Supper*. When he had nearly completed the work, with only the faces of Judas and Jesus yet to paint, he had a horrible conflict with another local painter. Out of spite he painted the face of his enemy as the face of Judas.

Can you imagine? How would you like to have your face represent Judas for all the world to see, for years to come?

However, as Leonardo tried to paint the face of Christ, he found himself stymied. He couldn't do it. It just wouldn't come together. He was unaccountably held back, frustrated, baffled.

Finally, he concluded that his problem was his own unforgiveness and bitterness toward his local rival. So he forgave the man and memorialized that forgiveness by blotting his likeness from the face of Judas. It was only then that the great Leonardo had the freedom to paint the face of Christ.

Are you trying to paint the face of Christ in your own life but find yourself stifled, frustrated, held back? Could there be unforgiveness somewhere? Perhaps it's an old rival or a family member. What about your dad? In my seminars for men held worldwide, I've found that 60 to 70 percent of my audiences indicate they didn't get what they needed from their fathers when they were growing up. As a result, many are hurt and bitter, living in perpetual unforgiveness.

If this is true of you, let me urge you to catapult that hurt. First, identify how you feel and then give it to the Lord. Perhaps it will help you to write down your hurt. Write a letter to your dad stating exactly how you feel about him. (Don't worry, you're not going to send it to him, and even if your father is deceased I recommend this exercise.) As you write, be honest—deal with whatever was at the heart of your pain (e.g., abuse, neglect, uninvolvement, perfectionism). Then actively forgive him. When you've done that, tear up the letter. If your dad is still living, begin to express your love and forgiveness in your interactions with him.

I know thousands of men who have gone through this process and come out with great liberty from the bonds of unforgiveness. I urge you to do the same whether it is your father or someone else you need to forgive.

Total Forgiveness

Remember, total forgiveness is absolutely essential if we are to have a positive feeling of committed affection toward others. As Christ forgave us, so should we forgive others (Colossians 3:13). How did Jesus Christ forgive us? Totally! Scripture says that as a result of our accepting Jesus Christ as our Savior and Lord, "Their sins and their lawless deeds I will remember no more" (Hebrews

10:17). Old Testament promises read, "As far as the east is from the west, so far has he removed our transgressions from us" (Psalm 103:12, NIV), and "Though your sins are as scarlet, they will be as white as snow" (Isaiah 1:18).

Jesus Christ has totally forgiven us. Therefore, we are to totally forgive other people. We do not forgive simply because we are trying to be nice, but because we ourselves already have been forgiven by Jesus Christ.

What is total forgiveness? When we truly forgive, three things will be true.

First, *we never dwell on the offense again.* If we completely forgive the offender, we consciously choose not to dwell on the issue again. When the Moravian missionaries first went to the Eskimos, they could not come up with a word in the Eskimo language for forgiveness, so they developed a compound one: *Issumagijoujungnainernik.* Translated, it means "not-being-able-to-think-about-it-anymore." Although the thought of the offense may come to mind sometimes, we exercise our will to turn from it immediately. We commit not to dwell on it.

Second, total forgiveness means *we will never again talk to anybody else about the forgiven offense.* How often we are tempted to talk behind people's backs, especially about how someone wronged us! But when we forgive someone, we pledge never to speak about what he or she did to us. We promise to keep our mouths shut when it comes to anything negative. Instead, we vow to speak only positively about that person.

Third, *we pledge not to bring up the offense to the offender ever again.* When we totally forgive someone, the offense is wiped away. It is as though he had never offended us at all. Therefore, we do not bring it up again, either verbally or nonverbally. We let it rest once and for all.

No Room for Revenge

Clearly, genuine affection gives no room for revenge. The following joke illustrates the sick mentality of revenge.

One day a man went to the hospital to visit his dying partner. Suddenly the dying man began to speak. "John," he said, "before I go I must confess some things. I know I am going to die. I want you to know that I robbed the firm of eighty thousand dollars several years ago. And I sold our secret formula to our competitors. Also, John, I am the fellow who supplied your wife with the evidence that got her a divorce and cost you that small fortune."

John murmured, "That's okay, old man, I'm the guy who poisoned you."

The story is humorous, but its principle is not. Too often we want revenge, but the consequences can be deadly to our own spirits.

It is painful to forgive a hurt, but much more painful not to. One day a little boy was asked what forgiveness was. He gave the following answer: "It is the odor that the flowers breathe when they are trampled on." What a striking picture! Forgiveness is the beautiful aroma of one person giving up his rights for the sake of another—and that is part of being a man.

"Hey," you say, "but that's not fair!"

Of course it isn't! Who said it was supposed to be fair? Look, my friend, if you want fair, then ask yourself this question: "What do I fairly deserve from God?" There's only one correct answer. The only thing we deserve from God is hell—an eternal separation from God. *That* is fair. We all have sinned big time and fallen short of God's ideal. But, thank the Lord, in the midst of our sinfulness God has fully forgiven us. Now *that's* not fair!

But it *is* grace. And it's what the Christian life is all about. It's not about trying to even the score, but about experiencing God's love and grace and then becoming vehicles to express His love to others. Wow! How liberating! His forgiving grace is the source of the positive emotions we can and should feel toward others.

2. Thinking Positive Thoughts

I've gone into detail about removing negative feelings because, if they linger in our lives, it is difficult for us to think positively. When we're free from those negative feelings, we are also free to think the best of one another, to give the benefit of the doubt, to look for the good in each other, to pray positively for one another.

God's Word tells us, "As he thinks within himself, so he is" (Proverbs 23:7). Actions, emotions, and thoughts are tremendously interdependent in every human being. I usually develop deep feelings when judgments first enter my mind. After emotions are more fully developed, certain actions begin to take place. The key, though, is my mind. We are commanded in Ephesians 4:23 to be "renewed in the spirit of your mind." Romans 12:2 tells us not to be conformed to the world; we are instead to be transformed by the renewing of our minds. If I want positive and affectionate feelings about other people, and if I want to act that way toward them, I must begin by rejecting my natural bent for the negative and deliberately think positive and affectionate thoughts about them. In 1 Corinthians 13, the classic passage on Christian love, the author says that love looks for the best in others (1 Corinthians 13:7).

I am, therefore, not to go around spotting and noting the negatives about others; I am to assume the best and focus on spotting and noting the positives!

Discernment

Let me explain, though, that I am not saying we are to lack discernment about other people. Obviously, people sometimes do make mistakes and act inappropriately. In Philippians we read,

> For God is my witness, how I long for you all with the affection of Christ Jesus. And this I pray, that your love may abound still more and more in real knowledge and all discernment, so that you may approve the things that are excellent, in order to be sincere and blameless until the day of Christ. (Philippians 1:8–10)

Paul admonishes the believers for whom he has great affection to develop knowledge and discernment so that they will know right from wrong. The assumption is that this discernment will come in relationship with people.

Assuming the Best

Have you ever walked into a room full of people, noticed one person in particular, and found yourself thinking, *That person doesn't like me*? As you watch the person standing in the corner talking with someone, your neurotic mind says he is talking about you, telling the other person something unpleasant about you. That springs from our incredible sense of insecurity and our penchant for assuming the worst instead of the best of others.

An embarrassing story illustrates my point. I was once asked to bring some chairs to a friend's house for a social gathering. He met me at the door and asked, "Where are the chairs?"

"Oh, I forgot!"

He looked me straight in the eye and said, "That figures!" Then he walked away.

I began to think, *What does he mean, "That figures"? He thinks I'm irresponsible! He thinks I can't be trusted! He doesn't like me! Who does he think he is?* Not much security there, eh?

But then God hit me right between the eyes. "Ron," He seemed to be saying, "You have only two options. One, you can forgive him for what he said and forget it, assuming the best. Or, two, you can go to him and ask him what he meant, believing the best about his intentions."

So out of cowardice, I forgave. I thought. However, several weeks later when I ran into my friend I asked him, "Do you remember a few weeks ago when I forgot to bring chairs to your house and you said, 'That figures'?"

"I shouldn't have said that!" he replied.

"That's what I thought. But since you did say it, I was wondering, what did you mean?"

"I had been in meetings all day long that day, and in every meeting someone had forgotten something." He said it just figured that his day would end the way it started.

But I had taken his statement as a personal attack on me. That kind of experience shows why we need to learn to think the best of people. We need to be discerning, but we also need to believe the best regarding people's motives. If we don't do that, there is no way we can have a strong affection for them.

A wise 101-year-old woman once said, "Everyone has what he believes are good reasons for doing whatever he does." So guys, let's be careful here! Let's avoid the tendency to think the worst. Let's give our families, teammates, coworkers, neighbors, and fellow believers the respect of believing the best about them instead! Let's be models of extending the benefit of the doubt.

We've studied the first two of six steps to building genuine affection for one another: feeling positive emotions and thinking positive thoughts. So, on a scale of 1 to 10, how do you rate yourself on each of these steps? In the next chapter, we'll look at four other steps to making genuine affection a more natural part of your relationships.

Action Steps

Identify someone about whom you need to feel positively and think positively. Write down the name of the person and the specific steps you need to take. Use the space below to record your commitments. Do it right now.

CHAPTER EIGHT

The Power of Affection
Part Two

More Steps toward Intense Christian Love

e affectionately desired you!" That is what Paul, Timothy, and Silvanus said to their fellow believers at Thessalonica. But it wasn't just their feelings or their thoughts, as we saw in the last chapter. It was what they did. They demonstrated their great affection for these people through their actions. That's why we're studying six action steps to building fond affection for one another.

We have established the first two steps, dealing with unforgiveness to pave the way for feeling positive emotions, then determining to think positive thoughts of each other, or always assuming the best. Using those as a base, let's move on to the other four steps. Here is the list again:

SIX STEPS TOWARD FOND AFFECTION

1. Feel Positive Emotions

2. Think Positive Thoughts

3. Focus on the Positive in People

4. Offer Positive Prayers

5. Speak Positive Words

6. Practice Positive Actions

3. Focusing on the Positive in People

As I shared earlier, when Mary and I toured the country in that 20-foot motor home with Alan and Theda, we found that after a while we began to irritate one another. We each had little habits that bothered the other three. Our eccentricities were all blown out of proportion as we lived under the magnifying glass of that exhausting trip.

Before long, though, we began to talk about some of these problems and decided to start concentrating on each other's strengths instead of our irritating habits. As we began to observe and appreciate the strengths of the other individuals, our affection for one another deepened. That was an invaluable lesson to me about the importance of focusing on the positive in people.

Another thing I learned is that weaknesses are often strengths blown out of proportion. For example, worry may be conscientiousness taken to an extreme. The tendency to be critical may be careful discernment pressed to an extreme. Anger may be a passionate commitment pushed to an extreme.

Our nature may be to focus on other people's weaknesses, but we can never develop a deep affection for them until we zero in on their strengths. A number of years ago, I moved a member of my staff from one position to another because he was not performing well in the first position. When we discussed his move, I explained that I recognized his strengths and felt they could be better utilized in a different area. He felt relieved rather than burdened. He had realized he was doing his job poorly but now he knew it was because the job maximized his weaknesses and minimized his strengths. He understood that he did not have to be good at everything, and he was now free to do what he was good at.

Had I focused only on my teammate's weaknesses in our discussion, I may have crushed his spirit. But since I emphasized that I wanted to place him in a spot where he could better use his ample strengths, he was able to make the move with dignity and excitement.

We need to develop the habit of discovering the positive qualities in people and amplifying those in our minds. "But, but, but…" you say. "You don't know what a jerk this guy is!"

Hello! Take a good look in the mirror.

Please don't get me wrong. Probably everyone in your orbit has down sides. But so do you. I certainly do. So let's not get hung up on weaknesses. They are a given. They're included in our sin nature, so they come with the package. Let's rise above it and concentrate instead on the positives. The impact will be stunning.

Take a minute right now and think of someone close to you (a spouse, child, friend, etc.). List below ten positive qualities you see in this person's life. Then concentrate for one week on these qualities. Focus on them several times a day, and watch what happens to your attitude and actions.

NAME: (optional)

1. *Forgiveness*
2. *strength*
3. *survivor*
4.
5.
6.
7.
8.
9.
10.

4. Offering Positive Prayers

I am impressed over and over again with Paul's constant emphasis on praying for other people with affection and from a positive viewpoint. Note the following Scriptures:

> For God is my witness, how I long for you all with the affection of Christ Jesus. And this I pray, that your love may abound still more and more in real knowledge and all discernment, so that you may approve the things that are excellent, in order to be sincere and blameless until the day of Christ; having been filled with the fruit of righteousness which comes through Jesus Christ, to the glory and praise of God. (Philippians 1:8–11)

> We give thanks to God, the Father of our Lord Jesus Christ, praying always for you. (Colossians 1:3)

> We give thanks to God always for all of you, making mention of you

in our prayers; constantly bearing in mind your work of faith and labor of love and steadfastness of hope in our Lord Jesus Christ in the presence of our God and Father, knowing, brethren beloved by God, His choice of you. (1 Thessalonians 1:2–4)

I thank my God always concerning you, for the grace of God which was given you in Christ Jesus, that in everything you were enriched in Him, in all speech and all knowledge, even as the testimony concerning Christ was confirmed in you, so that you are not lacking in any gift, awaiting eagerly the revelation of our Lord Jesus Christ, who shall also confirm you to the end, blameless in the day of our Lord Jesus Christ. God is faithful, through whom you were called into fellowship with His Son, Jesus Christ our Lord. (1 Corinthians 1:4–9)

We read repeatedly about Paul's concern and thankfulness for these people in his prayers. Note, for instance, how positively he prays in the above passage from 1 Corinthians, and yet, in all the rest of this letter, he castigates the people for their sinfulness. Immorality and improprieties were going on throughout the entire Corinthian church, and Paul confronts them on that, but in the meantime he offers positive prayers for them.

Why is that? I believe Paul saw these people for who they were in Jesus Christ: They had been bought with the price of His blood. Also, Paul realized these Corinthians were in the process of becoming holy. And finally, Paul had a deep affection for these people. Therefore, he could pray positively even while strongly admonishing them.

I urge you to pray the Scriptures for people. Constantly give thanks for them. Ask that God would bless them the way Paul and others pray in the above mentioned Scriptures—and watch what happens!

5. SPEAKING POSITIVE WORDS

God's Word commands:

Let no unwholesome word proceed from your mouth, but only such a word as is good for edification according to the need of the moment, that it may give grace to those who hear. (Ephesians 4:29)

We need to speak positively, affirming others if we want to build genuine fond affection for them.

But let's face it: Speaking positively about others is an uphill battle, for criticism, sarcasm, and cynicism seem to be national pastimes in America.

I am, quite frankly, tired of the negative and complaining spirit I see around me. I see it in the press, in the political world, among business leaders, in the culture at large—and in the church. That last one really hurts! I don't believe we Christians have the luxury of indulging in sarcastic attitudes. My brothers, we ought to be *for* things, not against things. We ought to provide solutions—after all, we have the answer Book and the power source.

In fact, did you know that your impact in life is in significant proportion to the sweetness of your spirit as revealed through a positive tongue? That's right. Your effect on others is in a great way determined by how positive and upbeat your attitude is. Philippians 2:14–15 points out the profound impact your tongue can have in the world around you:

> Do all things without grumbling or disputing; that you may prove yourselves to be blameless and innocent, children of God above reproach in the midst of a crooked and perverse generation, among whom you appear as lights in the world.

The American Institute of Family Relations did a survey in which parents were asked to record how many negative and how many positive comments they made to their children during a set period of time. The results: The parents criticized ten times for every one favorable thing they said! In another survey in Orlando, Florida, teachers were found to be 75 percent negative. And it was learned that from a teacher it takes four positive statements to offset the effects of one negative comment to a child.[1]

Isn't this tragic? How can we expect affection toward people to grow if we constantly criticize and discourage? Let me say again, I am not suggesting we never say negative things to people. Scripture makes it abundantly clear that we are to admonish, rebuke, warn, and beseech one another. Such statements, however, must be made in a constructive sense; they must be true, and they must be balanced by many more positive statements—apparently at least four times as many!

Every person must receive sincere affirmation and positive verbal reinforcement to be emotionally healthy. That is key to our demonstration of affection toward other people. In the book *Marriage Takes More Than Love,* Carole Mayhall says of her husband, "His refusal to belittle even my wildest ideas has been a great help on our journey to intimacy in our marriage."[2]

Coaching by affirmation was part of the genius of Harry Hopman as he

built an Australian dynasty in world tennis. He had a slow-footed boy he nick-
named "Rocket"; he had a weak, frail one he named "Muscles." They became
Rocket Rod Laver and Ken Muscles Rosewall, world tennis champions by
affirmation.

Jesus did the same thing. Remember the disciple who was impetuous and
rash, always putting his foot in his mouth? What did Jesus call him? *Petros:*
Peter, the Rock. Jesus didn't call him what he was, but what he would become.

Consider what Paul said to the Thessalonian believers, that he and his
compatriots had a "fond affection for them" and that "they had become very
dear to them." Paul verbalized their affection. He spoke lovingly and in an
uplifting manner. So must we if we are going to be effective Christian leaders.

Reflect now on your own communication style at home, at work, at
church. What percentage of the words that come out of your mouth are positive? What percentage would you say are negative? Write percentages in the
positive and negative columns that best describe your verbal behavior.

AREA	POSITIVE PERCENTAGE	NEGATIVE PERCENTAGE
Home	10	90
Work	85	15
Church	N/A	N/A

6. PRACTICING POSITIVE ACTIONS

Now, you may be tempted to say, "Jenson, you've gone too far. It's all right to
think and feel and see, but when you talk about *acting* affectionate toward
people, you really push me to the limit. After all, it's one thing to have emotion, but it's altogether another thing to show it!"

However, over and over again in Scripture, we read that we are to be affectionate through positive *actions.*

> Then he [Joseph] fell on his brother Benjamin's neck and wept; and
> Benjamin wept on his neck. And he kissed all his brothers and wept
> on them, and afterward his brothers talked with him. (Genesis
> 45:14–15)

And they began to weep aloud and embraced Paul, and repeatedly kissed him, grieving especially over the word which he had spoken, that they should see his face no more. (Acts 20:37–38)

Greet one another with a holy kiss. All the churches of Christ greet you. (Romans 16:16)

All the brethren greet you. Greet one another with a holy kiss. (1 Corinthians 16:20)

Greet one another with a kiss of love. Peace be to you all who are in Christ. (1 Peter 5:14)

These were not weak individuals. These were the Ephesian elders, the leaders of the church. Strong, emotional affection that is visibly seen through action is a vital part of Christian manhood.

I have noted in observing great leaders throughout my life that almost all of them seem to feel a freedom to touch. They may put their arm around an individual, or pat him on the back, or touch him in some other way, but they manage to demonstrate their affection. There are exceptions to this, of course, but those who penetrate the hearts of their followers and friends are often the ones who physically show affection, regardless of their personalities.

In my mind, one of the most godly men I've ever worked with is Dr. Bill Bright, whom I talked about earlier. Bill founded and leads one of the largest Christian ministries in the world. He is not naturally an extrovert, nor does he easily show his affection. Yet whenever I see him, he gives me a warm, loving hug. He is always patting people on the back or the shoulder. As a result of these warm actions, people love him and know that he truly loves them.

We all need to do the same. If we are to be strong men, we must be able to demonstrate affection. I encourage you to work on increasing your ability to put your arms around your friends, members of your family, your male coworkers. I challenge you to make a prolific use of handshaking and even embracing. Touching people reassures them of your acceptance and love, and it can be a powerful tool for breaking down barriers.

An important caution, however. Be careful about expressing your affection toward the opposite sex. Never, ever, get abusive or improper here. There are appropriate hugs and there are inappropriate hugs. This holds true even with our daughters. As a daughter grows older, what was appropriate changes. Just be careful!

How does this discussion about touching make you feel? Perhaps awkward, if you are like a lot of men. Many of us have not seen this kind of love manifested by other men in our lives. I am grateful that I did have a positive model—my dad. He was not only gentle but also openly affectionate. He knew how to hug his sons and his daughter appropriately. That served as a great demonstration for me, so I probably have been stronger in this realm over the years than a lot of other men.

Let me urge you to find a mentor who does this well and watch him. Learn from his behavior and then practice it. One of the best examples of a man of affectionate action I have ever seen is a businessman and longtime friend of mine, Arlis Priest. Arlis is a lover! He prays lovingly, he verbalizes love, he thinks love, he acts out love and affection. He and I, along with a number of other people, toured China one summer. As Arlis interacted with our Chinese tour guide, he would continually go to him, speak loving words to him, and hug him. Since there is tremendous austerity in any Chinese relationship outside the family, this kind of action was brand-new to our guide.

During our week-long stay, though, this young man began to open up and respond to Arlis. As Arlis was leaving on the last day, he squeezed Arlis's hand tightly and verbalized his love and appreciation for Arlis. I'm sure this encounter opened up a whole new dimension in the guide's life—a dimension that might never have been opened had it not been for Arlis Priest.

Among your circle of acquaintances, do you have a man who models both strength and fond affection? If not, look to the Scriptures and to the examples of Jesus, Paul, and others. But of course, finding a role model can take you only part way toward being the man God wants you to be. You must practice those positive actions yourself. Appropriate touching can transform lives through the fond affection it conveys.

A Lost Opportunity

One more caution, my friend! Do not allow the world system to trip you up here. The culture says, "Beware of touch or you'll seem odd," and "Be tough and distant, not open or intimate." It's easy to let the Satan-influenced culture win this battle. Please don't! Learn from my personal experience here.

Some years ago, my son Matt was elected Homecoming King at his high school. The school had several thousand students and though Matt wasn't a football player (the usual nominee) or a student body officer, he was crowned king. I believe it was because he poured his life into the kids at his school. Matt did exactly what Paul and Timothy and Silvanus did, and he was honored for his affectionate spirit.

During halftime of the homecoming football game, the Homecoming

Court was presented to the crowd. Each member of the court was to walk down the 50-yard line from the visitors' side to the home side, accompanied by his or her parents. There were hundreds of people in the stands—students, faculty, administration, and other parents. It was a big night, probably the biggest in my son's life.

As Matt's turn came, his mother and I turned the corner and began walking down the 50-yard line with him. Mary put her arm through Matt's arm and Matt reached out to grab my hand. Well, I thought he was kidding. I mean, he was a high schooler, and surely he didn't want to hold my hand in front of all of these people! So I put my hand in my pocket and we finished our procession.

Matt was crowned and the evening was perfect, right? Wrong!

The next day Mary came to me and said, "Honey, do you know how deeply you hurt Matt last night?"

"What?" I was shocked.

She went on to tell me that when Matt reached out to me, he had really wanted to hold my hand. When I pushed her for specifics she said, "This was Matt's biggest night ever. He has witnessed of his faith to so many of these kids, teachers, and parents. They all want what we have as a family. They so admire his relationship with his family and especially with you, his dad. He wanted to demonstrate to everyone there how great that love and affection is. Honey, you robbed him of that honor."

Shame on me! I had let the world system push me into hurting this young man I love so deeply. I went to Matt immediately and apologized. He was gracious and forgave me. But we will never have that moment back.

How many moments like that have slipped through your fingers because you let something other than the Lord guide you? Let's break with the culture and be men of powerful affection. Let's show society what godly men who really care "look like." Let's change our world.

Action Steps

Choose a family member or a close friend and focus this week on using the four skills we talked about in this chapter. Write down what you can do specifically to practice each of these skills.

Focusing on the Positive: Good morals - exc. attitude -

Offering Positive Prayers:

Speaking Positive Words:

Practicing Positive Actions:

Now, do it!

CHAPTER NINE

EFFECTIVE
COMMUNICATION

Secrets of Clear Understanding

You said it; you understood it; you thought it was clear. But the other person just didn't get it!

Someone has said that the natural result of communication is confusion. Often many of us could sum up our efforts in that realm with: "I know you believe you understand what you think I said, but I'm not sure you realize that what you heard is not what I meant."

Confusion in communication is illustrated by these actual statements made on automobile accident reports:

- A truck backed through my windshield into my wife's face.
- A pedestrian hit me and went under my car.
- The guy was all over the road. I had to swerve a number of times before I hit him.
- I had been driving for forty years when I fell asleep at the wheel and had an accident.
- I was on my way to the doctor with rear end trouble when my universal joint gave way, causing me to have an accident.
- To avoid hitting the bumper of the car in front I struck the pedestrian.
- An invisible car came out of nowhere, struck my car, and vanished.
- I was sure the old fellow would never make it to the other side of the road when I struck him.
- The pedestrian had no idea which direction to run, so I ran over him.
- I saw a slow-moving, sad-faced old gentleman as he bounced off the roof of my car.

- The indirect cause of the accident was a little guy in a small car with a big mouth.[1]

Clear communication is another skill we must sharpen if we want to be effective Christian men. In this chapter we'll look again to Paul as our model. As he and his coworkers imparted the gospel to the Thessalonians (see 1 Thessalonians 2:8), they knew how to relate truth in a clear, understandable manner.

BEING HEARD

Think for a minute about this question: What is communication?

The best definition I have found is: "Communication is a process (verbal and nonverbal) of sharing information with another person in such a way that the other person understands what you are saying."[2]

Another way to define this concept is that I communicate when the picture in the mind of the person to whom I am speaking is the same as the picture in my mind. If it is not, I have not communicated clearly.

But, contrary to the simplicity of this definition, the act of communication is incredibly tough. William James has said, "The most immutable barrier in nature is between one man's thought and another." Someone else has said, "You will never know exactly what I mean and I'll never know exactly what you mean."

Sometimes the dynamics involved in the communication process make it even more difficult. I realized this one summer when I spoke to a number of large church groups in Korea. I would speak in sentences that were as brief as possible, and my interpreter would translate. Although the response seemed positive, I never really knew how well I was getting my ideas across.

My feelings about communicating through that interpreter mirror those summed up by James Evans: "To work through an interpreter is like hacking one's way through a forest with a feather." Consider this instance of interpretation. When the phrase "out of sight, out of mind" was first translated by computers into Russian and then retranslated into English, it became "invisible maniac"!

HOW COMMUNICATION HAPPENS

Communication begins when one person speaks and an idea is formed in the mind of the listener. The listener's human radar gathers data from all surroundings—what is being said, who is saying it, the situation they are in, his own past experience, how he feels that day, his self-image, and an array of other possible filters. All this influences him to assign a meaning to what he hears. He then forms a responding message in his mind and sends that message back to the speaker, who then goes through the same process. Feedback can be verbal or nonverbal, the same as the messages going out.

We all know from experience how confusing sharing information can be, how vital it is to understand each other, and how difficult it can be to assign the right meaning to what we hear. Every time we communicate, many types of messages are sent. When you add to that the various experiences and personalities through which we interpret the messages we hear, you see why we have such difficulty in understanding each other.

I do not want to leave you, though, with the thought that good communication is impossible. It's challenging, but we can do it!

Is communication a strong suit or a weak one for you? Think about a recent discussion with your spouse or a good friend. Did you actually understand what that person was saying? Did she or he really understand you? What do you think you could have done to improve the exchange?

To help you answer those questions and grow in your personal communications skills, let's look at some specific fundamentals of effective communication.

Principles of Effective Communication

1. Watch Your Tongue

In an earlier chapter we talked about the importance of watching what we say. We can do more harm with an inappropriately stated thought than we might ever have imagined. Friendships have been destroyed by just one ill-chosen phrase.

Sir Walter Raleigh once stated, "It is observed in the course of worldly things that men's fortunes are oftener made by their tongues than by their virtues, and more men's fortunes overthrown thereby than by vices."

But just as a word improperly said can be destructive, a word fitly spoken can give new delights, make a plain person beautiful, heal bruises, soothe agitated tempers, give hope to despondent souls, and point the way to God.

Scripture clearly defines for us the proper use of the tongue:

Therefore, laying aside falsehood, speak truth, each one of you, with his neighbor, for we are members of one another. Be angry, and yet do not sin; do not let the sun go down on your anger, and do not give the devil an opportunity. Let him who steals steal no longer; but rather let him labor, performing with his own hands what is good, in order that he may have something to share with him who has need.

Let no unwholesome word proceed from your mouth, but only such a word as is good for edification according to the need of the moment, that it may give grace to those who hear. And do not grieve the Holy Spirit of God, by whom you were sealed for the day of redemption.

Let all bitterness and wrath and anger and clamor and slander be put away from you, along with all malice. And be kind to one another, tender-hearted, forgiving each other, just as God in Christ also has forgiven you. (Ephesians 4:25–32)

SPEAK ONLY WHAT IS TRUE, EDIFYING, AND KIND

Three points from this passage are pertinent to our study of communication.

First, *our words are to be true.* In verse 25, Paul instructs each of us to put aside lies and tell only things that are true. We live in a time of tremendous duplicity. Even as well-intentioned Christian men, it is easy to become entangled in subtle lies or even overt ones. It may help you to review and commit to some practical guidelines:

- Avoid half-truths. For example, don't say, "The truck hit my car" when you had an accident and it was actually your fault.
- Distinguish between fact and opinion. Don't state something as reality when it is simply your opinion. Use the phrase "I think" or "In my opinion."
- Be careful about absolute statements. For example, "You never talk to me" or "I don't have anything to wear" are not true statements. They are exaggerations and, in essence, are lies. When you think about it, "never" and "always" are rarely true.
- Be truthful about yourself. Admit when you are wrong or when you can't do something.
- Be careful of "white lies." For the Christian, no lie is acceptable. You may think a little lie may help someone, but in the long run that is never true.

A second key point from this passage is that *we are to say only things that are necessary.* As men of God, we're admonished to steer clear of unwholesome words and discussions and to speak only words that will "give grace" to the hearer. We should speak to build someone up or to meet a need. Unwholesome or degrading words do not edify others or honor our Lord.

So often we speak when we shouldn't! Perhaps we would all do well to live by the New England proverb: "Don't talk unless you can improve the silence."

The third point we can draw from the above Scripture passage is that *we are to be kind.* The last two verses of the passage instruct us to get rid of the negative, hurtful things—the wrath, anger, slander, and malice.

Back in my teen years, I had a stupid habit of putting down people I particularly liked. For some reason I thought my swift put-downs showed how clever I was. I recall saying to a girl, "You know what I like about you?"

"No, tell me!" she replied.

"Nothing! Absolutely nothing!"

I thought I was funny, but she didn't. She was deeply hurt by those unkind words.

The heart of all this discussion about the tongue is clear: We should always be truthful; we should speak only when we can encourage or uplift people; and we should always be kind.

2. Listen

The second principle of good communication is also vital: We must listen, genuinely listen, to what people say. We need to remember the words of Polonius in *Hamlet:* "Give every man thine ear, but few thy voice." You will never understand another person's perspective unless you listen carefully to him. Without understanding, real communication cannot take place.

We are to be "quick to hear, slow to speak" (James 1:19). This is radically different from how most of us behave. My tendency (and that of most men I know) is to try to fix things. This is especially true when speaking to my wife. But she seldom wants me to fix her problem; she simply wants me to listen, understand, and empathize.

We men are so different from women in this arena. It is almost instinctive. How many times have you wanted to fix your wife's problem and make it go away without truly giving her your time, attention, and listening ear?

When Mary and I speak at Family Life conferences, we often introduce ourselves by quoting a poem Mary wrote that reflects our differences. See if you can relate to it.

THE EAGLE AND THE CAT

I am the eagle.
> *I am the cat.*
Together we live in
a San Diego "flat,"
with a daughter, a son,
one dog and a pool,

and a view from the hills
of the town and a school.

> As an eagle I fly o'er the
> land and I look
> to see the big picture.
>> *I study my books.*
> I like to be free, to
> determine my day
> to swoop close and
> personal
> or sail high and away.
>> *I, on the other hand,*
>> *like comfort and*
>> *warmth,*
>> *like fireplaces and*
>> *blankets*
>> *and tea by the*
>> *hearth—*
>> *I, too, value freedom*
>> *but don't make me*
>> *face*
>> *the outside—take*
>> *care of me,*
>> *then give me some*
>> *space.*

> People intrigue me, if I
> choose when and where,
> and if when I'm ready I can
> escape to the air.
>> *I like to know*
>> *people're there when*
>> *I need them.*
>> *But I hate to cook*
>> *so don't ask me to*
>> *feed them!*

We do love the world.
Our hearts melt with care
when we're faced with the picture of

pain and despair.
But somehow when given
a choice for the night,
> *To curl up with some friends*
or go out for a flight,
or to stay home together
with no one around—
we'll choose the latter and we
can't be found.

> As an eagle I work hard
> then sit back and float,
>> *As a cat I'm*
>> *contemplative*
>> *spending time on my*
>> *coat.*
>> *I like quiet*
>> *days with*
>> *naught on my plate*
>> *but thinking and*
>> *reading…*
> Quiet I hate!
> I turn on the tube,
> or put in CDs,
> get sound in the
> background—
>> *Drives me to my*
>> *knees.*
> It gives me energy
> Keeps me in the pink
> Just let me DO!
>> *Just let me THINK!*
>> *I love rainy days*
>> *when*
>> *everyone's gone*
>> *and everything's*
>> *quiet*
> I love the sun!
> I love excitement,
> and challenge and speed,

While I love routine
and nursing my
needs,
                    with a small group of
friends whose values
I share.
Just give me freedom!
Just give me air!

Our nearly grown children
are a great satisfaction,
                    but I take it safely
and I like to take action!
                    I want to carry them
                    safe in my jaws;
I want to push them from
the nest with my claws.
                    I want to love them
                    and take all their
                    pain;
I want to love them and
see their lives gain
by the struggles they go
through
                    I guess I do, too.
                    But it's so much
                    harder for me
                    than for you.

We're learning that both ways have
a place in the rearing
of the young that God gives us
and hope that they're hearing
that we pray and we struggle
to bring them up right
                    with a cat's
                    sensitivity
and an eagle's free flight.

                    Perhaps you can tell

that I tend to get
low...
I was depressed once,
a long time ago.

He makes me laugh
when I'm
under the pile.
She makes me stop and
slow down for a while.

He takes me for
walks
and listens to my
heart.
She reminds me
that I need to take part
in the lives of others
and come down from the
crags—
give my back and my
wings
to others who sag.

As a cat I take
comfort in
maintaining control,
in planning the
schedule—
after all, that's my
role.
As an eagle I like
spontaneous life.
I ride on the wind,
have the time of my life.
I know I can do it

while I'm never quite
sure,
but together we're solid, committed,
and you're

> sure to see us
> gliding around
>   I in the sky,
>   *I on the ground.*
>   *Secure in his*
>   *strength*
>   buoyed by her grace,
> hands and arms linked,
> running the race.
>   © Mary Jenson

This idea of differences was driven home to me some time ago when Mary asked me to go out for lunch to discuss some issues she was facing. We parked ourselves at the table of a local restaurant near our home.

Mary began by asking me a number of questions concerning the issue at hand, and I started answering her questions. I mean, that is what she wanted, right? No! She wanted me to listen.

In fact, as I began to share my great insight with her, she patted my hand (I knew I was in trouble then) and said, "Honey, I don't want you to answer my questions. I just want you to listen."

Now, I must tell you that I said to myself, *Why is she asking me questions if she doesn't want answers?* But I have learned enough about communication to know I needed to shut up and simply seek to understand what she was thinking—and feeling.

So I spent the next two hours listening and asking a few clarifying questions such as, "Honey, when you say this, do you mean..." or "Help me understand better what you are feeling."

When we got through (remember, I made no comments and gave no answers) Mary leaned over the table, looked at me with those beautiful puppy-dog eyes, lifted her hands to my cheeks, planted a big kiss on my lips, and said adoringly, "Honey, thank you, thank you. This has been the best discussion we have ever had."

That's right, the best "discussion." This was a discussion? Of course it was, and she felt that way because for once I kept my fix-it mind in check, bit my lip, and listened. This is what our wives (and dare I say anyone with whom we share the bond of Christian love) need from us most in communication. Not the Answer Man or Mr. Fix-It, but a good listener.

3. Put the Speaker at Ease

Establish and maintain a receptive atmosphere in the discussion. Don't give the impression that you are ready to jump on every word spoken.

Sometimes our fix-it mindset hurts this process. Though you need to build into people, confront them appropriately, and be forthright, you must also help people open up. This happens as they know you authentically care for them. Remember the trusty adage: "People will not care how much you know until they know how much you care."

I've found one of the best ways for me to put the speaker at ease is to pray for that person and ask God for wisdom to understand and meet his or her needs.

This approach is best illustrated through the definition of friendship that many of us on the Promise Keepers faculty have used: "A true friend is someone who knows all about me, loves me for who I am, and has no plans for my immediate improvement." That says it all, doesn't it?

4. Don't Avoid Controversy

Avoiding controversy is impossible. Scripture demands that Christian men maintain a spirit of unity, but it does not dictate that we agree on everything. We are bound to disagree. We simply need to disagree in a loving way. Therefore, don't try to dodge disagreement or controversy; simply handle it appropriately.

I know it is easy to run away from this, but as leaders we just can't. In a recent meeting some of the principals in one of our companies had some major disagreements (by the way, no big deal) and were trying to work through them. It was tough. We experienced everything from the "I'm going to take my ball and go home" syndrome to harsh words and defensiveness to the silent treatment. One of the brothers complained about a relationship problem in the group but wouldn't open up until we simply begged him to do so. But we kept applying the "speak the truth in love" model, and when we finally worked through the issues we were more committed to our cause and to one another than ever.

When a controversy comes up, remember the male tendency is to either "stuff it" (bury our feelings or views), or "strike out" (get upset, yell, demand, argue, pout). But both of these are inappropriate. The key is to speak the truth in love. Be truthful and be loving. Always!

5. Watch Your Emotions

There are a number of ways to keep your emotions in check—and we'll look at them in the next chapter. For now, let's just underscore the basic tenet that we must be sure we do not blow up and hurl our emotions at other people. This is absolutely devastating to quality communication as well as to the relationship itself.

6. Remove Distractions

When you're talking with someone, don't doodle, or look around, or allow other distractions to interfere. Concentrate on the individual. I am impressed by former U.S. Senator Bill Armstrong. Whenever I met with this incredibly busy man, he gave me his total attention and made me feel very, very important. I've noticed he does that with everyone. What a great example of artful communication.

7. Empathize with the Person

Try to put yourself in the other person's shoes. Try to see the subject from the other person's perspective. That is sometimes very difficult to do, but it is essential to empathic listening, the first key to effective communication.

I unpacked this concept earlier when we addressed the importance of listening. But you'll want to be sure you truly feel with your friend. He needs to know you genuinely understand where he is coming from.

8. Be Patient

Effective communication doesn't happen quickly or by schedule. Give yourself plenty of time to listen without interruption. Do not become upset or impatient if the conversation isn't as bottom line as you would like. This person needs you right now. Don't allow yourself to jump to any conclusions, but patiently seek to understand what he's saying.

9. Ask Questions

Asking questions encourages the person and shows him you are both interested and listening. Further, the responses will help you understand the other person's point of view. You might ask a question like, "Could you clarify that last point?" or "What do you mean by that?" or "How did that make you feel?"

With all we've said about clear communication and the difficulties entailed, you may be tempted to not even try. But as we have seen from some of the illustrations in this chapter, even *no* communication speaks loudly. Refusing to share thoughts or feelings shows neither strength nor the ability to stay calm and in control. Instead, lack of communication indicates that a man fears revealing himself lest he may not be accepted. It reveals a man more concerned about a propped-up image of masculinity than about other people and how they can become all God wants them to be.

Good communication involves hard work. By taking each of these skills, one by one, and building them into a new habit, you will be more effective in promoting clear understanding wherever you go. Just as a good baseball player hones his basic skills of batting, catching, and throwing, so you can sharpen your skills of communicating. The key: practice, practice, practice. Ask a brother to pray for you and to hold you accountable as you begin working on each skill at home and then as you move into the church and the workplace. Remember, if you can practice consistently for twenty-one days, you will begin to ingrain the habit.

Remember also, feed the good new habit and starve the old bad habit. The more you "discipline yourself for godliness," the more you will experience and enjoy your new way of life.

Action Steps

Evaluate your strengths and weaknesses in the area of communication on the following chart using the (2 = weak; 8 = strong) scale. Choose one skill to focus on this week and begin to turn it into a habit—and practice, practice, practice!

1. Watch your tongue	2 4 6 8
2. Listen	2 4 6 8
3. Put the speaker at ease	2 4 6 8
4. Don't avoid controversy	2 4 6 8
5. Watch your emotions	2 4 6 8
6. Remove distractions	2 4 6 8
7. Empathize with the person	2 4 6 8
8. Be patient	2 4 6 8
9. Ask questions	2 4 6 8

Write out your action plan now. What will you do? When? Where? With whom? How?

CHAPTER TEN

GIVING
YOUR LIFE

Setting Aside Our Natural Selfishness

My wife was sick the other day and really needed my help. Mary asks very little of me, but she does need me when she is sick. I had planned to go out and play basketball with my friends, so when Mary asked me to stay in, I balked—I needed the exercise.

The fact of the matter is, exercise wasn't my motivation, fun was. What a lousy response on my part. Yet this hesitation is nothing unusual. Selfishness is common, even among Christians.

Perhaps that's why the apostle Paul underscored the importance of giving of ourselves, of setting aside our natural selfishness to focus on the needs of others. As he wrote in 1 Thessalonians 2:8, "We were well-pleased to impart to you not only the gospel of God but also our own lives." The word for "life" here is the Greek word *psyche,* or soul. Paul is referring to giving our entire being. In essence, he's saying, "We imparted to you all of us—we gave you our hearts and feelings and emotions and thoughts and lives."

Paul and his coworkers not only shared the truth with the Thessalonians and showed affectionate love toward them, but they also gave of themselves to these people. They demonstrated the standard articulated by Jesus in John 15:13: "Greater love has no one than this, that one lay down his life for his friends."

What does imparting our lives this way, this kind of total sharing, entail? Three essential practices stand out to me: getting involved, being transparent, and learning to listen.

GETTING INVOLVED

One of the great problems of our day is apathy. Most people simply don't care about other people. George Bernard Shaw has said, "The worst sin toward our fellow creatures is not to hate them, but to be indifferent to them; that is the essence of inhumanity."

Edmund Burke remarked, "The only thing necessary for the triumph of evil is for good men to do nothing."

And Helen Keller once said, "Science may have found a cure for most evils but it has found no remedy for the worst of them all—the apathy of human beings."

In our world of selfish apathy, one of the best, most obvious ways to give our life to others is to get involved in their lives, to demonstrate beyond mere words that we care. But many of us who relish our independence have trouble in this area. Do you really get involved in the lives of those around you? Or do you even care? I know that sounds harsh, but believe me, I grapple with it myself. I like my space! I like my independence! As a result, I find myself leaning toward satisfying myself much more than getting involved in the lives of others.

Just last night, my son called me from Wheaton College where he serves as the student director of the World Christian Fellowship (a campus ministry involving 700 to 800 students). He asked that Mary and I pray for their group meeting that night. An African Christian leader was going to speak, and the members of Matt's leadership team were believing God for great things. He simply wanted our prayer support.

What struck me about myself was how little I wanted to be bothered. Oh, don't get me wrong—we did pray. We believed God with Matt. But I admit I sure didn't feel like it. And there was an unhealthy ambivalence inside me concerning what God might do. That comes with my sin baggage, and I don't like it. You shouldn't either. We need to get involved—to really care at a mental, emotional, and physical level for those around us.

As I seek to be less selfish and more deeply involved with others, I've found that consciously taking these steps helps me break out of the apathy trap: praying for those around me, remembering what God has done for me, verbalizing my interest and concern, and taking initiative to do something for someone. (Even random acts of kindness will propel us in the direction of making caring involvement a way of life.)

BEING TRANSPARENT

Scripture clearly states that our lives are an open book to God:

> For the word of God is living and active and sharper than any two-edged sword, and piercing as far as the division of soul and spirit, of

both joints and marrow, and able to judge the thoughts and intentions of the heart. And there is no creature hidden from His sight, but all things are open and laid bare to the eyes of Him with whom we have to do. (Hebrews 4:12–13)

What does the writer of Hebrews mean when he says the Word of God "pierces"? He declares that God penetrates our facade, our mask. God wants to touch the innermost part of our hearts. He wants to sift out and analyze our thoughts and intentions, what we are reflecting upon and feeling. We are, in effect, absolutely naked before Him, so nothing is hidden from Him.

Yet He waits for us to ask Him to point out areas in our lives that need to be brought into conformity to His will. In Psalm 139:23–24, David writes, "Search me, O God, and know my heart; try me and know my anxious thoughts; and see if there be any hurtful way in me, and lead me in the everlasting way." David cried out to God to reveal to him anything that would hinder his intimate relationship with the Father.

Not only is God interested in our being open, or transparent, with Him, but He is also interested in our being that way toward other people. Scripture offers many illustrations of our need for honesty and vulnerability with one another. In the book of 2 Corinthians, for instance, Paul writes freely about some of the struggles he has had. He says at one point, "We do not want you to be unaware, brethren, of our affliction which came to us in Asia, that we were burdened excessively, beyond our strength, so that we despaired even of life" (2 Corinthians 1:8). In the same vein, James says in James 5:16, "Confess your sins to one another, and pray for one another, so that you may be healed."

What Transparency Is Not

A word of caution here: Transparency is not unloading all the dirt in your life. Indeed, Scripture says, "It is disgraceful even to speak of the things which are done by them in secret" (Ephesians 5:12). Neither is transparency an excuse to share all your emotional problems or to wear them on your sleeve. Sharing negative thoughts and feelings in the name of honesty is not openness.

I recently had a discussion with a friend who wanted to learn to be transparent but was having some real struggles. I let her know that her attempt to be honest did not mean hiding the emotional problems, but neither did it mean letting everyone know how difficult things were or letting her negative emotions affect her work. This goes beyond transparency to the point of whining, complaining, and pulling other people down.

What Transparency Is

Healthy transparency, on the other hand, is a willingness to admit that we're human, that we struggle with problems and temptation, tempered with an underlying assurance that God is sovereign and at work for our best interests. It acknowledges that life can be tough, but that in spite of it all we can praise God by faith that He's working it all together for our good. It points those around us to His majesty and to the fact that He is Lord.

We find a good example of such transparency in the New Testament when we read what Paul writes to the people of Corinth:

> But we have this treasure in earthen vessels, that the surpassing greatness of the power may be of God and not from ourselves; we are afflicted in every way, but not crushed; perplexed, but not despairing; persecuted, but not forsaken; struck down, but not destroyed; always carrying about in the body the dying of Jesus, that the life of Jesus also may be manifested in our body. For we who live are constantly being delivered over to death for Jesus' sake, that the life of Jesus also may be manifested in our mortal flesh. So death works in us, but life in you....
>
> Therefore we do not lose heart, but though our outer man is decaying, yet our inner man is being renewed day by day. For momentary, light affliction is producing for us an eternal weight of glory far beyond all comparison, while we look not at the things which are seen but at the things which are not seen, for the things which are seen are temporal, but the things which are not seen are eternal. (2 Corinthians 4:7–12, 16–18)

We saw this passage in chapter 6, but we need it again here. Note the intense pressure and pain Paul experienced, the freedom with which he communicates that pain, and especially the fact that in the midst of the difficulty he comes out with a jubilant statement about how God is giving him the ultimate victory. That's healthy transparency!

There are two specific things we can do to develop the kind of transparency Paul models. First, we can realize we are not yet perfect and, with this acknowledgment, start to deal with the normal male fear of being open. Second, we can learn how to better share our feelings, admittedly a tough practice for many of us.

Pretending to Be Perfect

Many of us try to pretend we are perfect. Like animals who camouflage themselves so well they blend into their surroundings, we try to camouflage our feelings so we won't be hurt, rejected, or criticized. Paul Tournier has said, "We conceal our persons behind a protective barrier; we let it be seen only through the bars; we display certain of its aspects, others we carefully hide."[1]

Have you ever noticed how a child tends to be spontaneous and absolutely honest? If children don't like what you say, they tell you so. They share how they feel, their hurts as well as their joys. As a child begins to grow up, though, he learns that his actions can sometimes lead to unpleasant results. He learns to keep to himself things that are painful to him or that cause pain in other people. He begins to present himself to other people in such a way that they will believe what he wants them to believe about him. Sidney Jourard calls this "the poker game of society, in which we bluff one another with our multitude of masks." We enclose ourselves in a protective armor.

Often we not only deceive other people, but through continual practice we end up deceiving ourselves. In *I, Too, Am Man,* James Dolby describes this predicament:

> Once in a while we want to stop playing this game of make believe, but when we try to stop we are confronted with the depressing and startling truth: We cannot stop. When we ask ourselves a question, "Who am I?" we don't know, and we find that no matter how hard we struggle, we are not able to find out. We are caught in the pattern of dishonesty—to be honest with ourselves is not natural.[2]

When Moses received the Ten Commandments, he covered his face as he came down from the mountain (see Exodus 34:33). He had seen the glory of the Lord, and he wore a veil because he did not want the people to see the glory of God departing from him (2 Corinthians 3:14). Today, many of us live behind a veil. Sometimes people come to know Jesus Christ in a personal way and they feel very "spiritual" for a while. After a period of time, however, that feeling wanes, but the Christian discovers that, if he acts as those in his Christian community expect him to act, he will be accepted. He can even rise to a position of leadership. Inside, though, he feels a great void. He is hollow, empty, defeated, and frustrated. He doesn't even know who he is.

God doesn't want this kind of duplicity. He wants men who will say with the apostle Paul:

> Having therefore such a hope, we use great boldness in our speech, and are not as Moses, who used to put a veil over his face that the sons of Israel might not look intently at the end of what was fading away....
>
> But whenever a man turns to the Lord, the veil is taken away.

Now the Lord is the Spirit; and where the Spirit of the Lord is, there is liberty. But we all, with unveiled face beholding as in a mirror the glory of the Lord, are being transformed into the same image from glory to glory, just as from the Lord, the Spirit. (2 Corinthians 3:12–13, 16–18)

We don't wear a veil anymore because the glory of God within us is not departing. At least, it should not be. Rather, it should be increasing as we are slowly transformed into the image of Christ. People may be able to see our failures, but we ought not to be afraid of that. We don't need to pretend perfection. We can learn through our struggles as we move progressively toward a likeness of Jesus Christ.

I have been continuously liberated as I read what the apostle Paul said to Timothy. He gave him instructions on how he ought to live as the leader in the church where he ministered; and then he said, "Take pains with these things; be absorbed in them, so that your progress may be evident to all" (1 Timothy 4:15). For our progress to be evident to everyone means people notice we are not the same person today that we were yesterday. We need not hide the fact that we are not perfect. As we gain the ability to be honest before people, we are on the way to healthy transparency and growth.

Let's do a reality check. When it comes to being open, where do you stand? Are you more transparent or more a "hider"? Check yes or no to each of these questions to gauge your openness.

QUESTION	YES	NO
1. Do I pretend to be something in public that I am not in private?	X	
2. Do I find it difficult to share my inner feelings?	X	
3. Am I without someone in my life with whom I can share anything?		X
4. Do I normally respond to criticism defensively?	X	
5. Do I have secrets I won't tell anyone?	X	
6. Am I more concerned with my outward appearance than my inward character?		X
7. Do I fear rejection if I open up to others?		X

Sharing Your Feelings

When you start sharing with someone, you usually choose one of five distinct levels of information: *clichés, gossip, opinions, feelings,* and *complete honesty.*

1. *Clichés.* Clichés, the shallow level of verbal interchange, involve saying something out of habit without thinking about it. The question, "How are you?" for example, elicits the automatic reply, "Fine, thank you," whether we are or not.

Sometimes when I call someone on the phone and merely say "Hi," they reply, "Fine. How are you?"

When that happens, I always want to respond, "I didn't even ask how you were!"

I understand, though, that the comment is a habit. People do not always think about what they are saying; sometimes they just say things.

However, clichés are not necessarily bad. Imagine if every time someone stopped you on the street and asked how you were, you really went deep with that person—you'd never get to work! It's okay to communicate in small talk at times—just not all the time.

2. *Gossip.* It is easy to gossip because, by talking about other people, we hide ourselves. Ironically, we also reveal a great deal about ourselves when we gossip. We are telling the other person, for instance, that we can't be trusted, also that we have some internal need to place ourselves above other people by speaking negatively about them.

Whenever I am tempted to say something unfavorable about someone, I like to think through Ephesians 4:29–32 (quoted in the last chapter). In light of this passage, asking yourself the following questions will gain you progressive victory over gossip:

Is it *true?*

Is it *kind?*

Is it *necessary?*

3. *Opinions.* Sharing opinions, what we really think inside, indicates that we are beginning to trust the other person. This is not always easy. For example, have you ever noticed how difficult it is to disagree with people? We fear that our opinions will be rejected, and if people reject our opinions, they are really rejecting us.

However, when two people share their ideas and opinions with each other a relationship can begin to develop. But be advised, it takes a pretty positive-minded person to take the initiative needed to get that started.

4. *Feelings.* Our feelings are our most intensely felt understanding of life around us and within us. Once we start to share feelings we open up the

fourth level, a deeper level of communication. We begin to tell people what we are really like inside.

When you share your hurts with another person, when you become vulnerable, that person bonds with you. He won't reject you or think less of you, but he will reach out to you. You see, he has his own disappointments and plenty of his own demons to face. People can be remarkably understanding and supportive when given a chance.

My son Matt recently asked me to pray for him and hold him accountable for a habit he is trying to change. He was vulnerable and open with me, and I loved him all the more for it. By the way, it also made me desire all the more to be transparent with him.

Try opening yourself up. Share your joys and frustrations, your victories and defeats, your insights and questions. And watch what happens to your level of relationships.

5. *Complete honesty.* The deepest level of personal interchange is the most personal and is reserved for the closest and most intimate relationships.

An old English word for communication is "intercourse." We usually think of intercourse in sexual terms, but it really means the coming together of two people. It has been used to describe verbal exchange for hundreds of years. God's desire for Christians is that we become one in thinking and feeling with each other.

This complete honesty is communication at its ultimate level, and we certainly cannot have it with everybody all the time. But we ought to be continually moving toward it. Otherwise we can become superficial individuals who hide behind clichés, gossip, or opinions, simply passing time in our interactions with people without ever building meaningful relationships.

At what level do you communicate with God, yourself, your wife, your children, and other Christian friends? Evaluate what percentage of your time is spent at each of the five levels in the following areas.

RELATIONSHIP	CLICHÉS	GOSSIP	OPINIONS	FEELINGS	COMPLETE HONESTY
God					100
Self			20	40	40
Marriage	20		40	30	10
Children			50	10	40
Other friends			40	40	20

LEARNING TO LISTEN

I know I addressed this briefly in an earlier chapter, but it's important to highlight it here as well: One of the best ways to give ourselves to others is to become skillful, empathic listeners.

During a conversation, our minds can comprehend many times the amount of information we hear. Therefore, it's very easy to let our minds wander. I have a terrible time with that.

When our children were small, Mary sometimes felt pushed to the breaking point when she wanted to leave the children home with me and had to give me instructions. Her standard approach was to come up to me as she was leaving the house, put her two hands on my chubby little cheeks, and say to me, "Look at me. Watch my lips." Only when she was sure I was listening did she give me her instructions. Then she'd say, "Now repeat what I said to you."

This ritual is a standing joke in our home, and yet its practice did slow me down enough to listen. Mary knows how often she has asked me to do something and I have totally forgotten about it. In fact, at times I never heard her in the first place!

We often think we are listening when we are merely hearing words the other person says. Let me suggest what good listening is. When I really listen to somebody, I become absorbed in the individual and what he or she is saying and feeling. It's more than basic intellectual comprehension. I attempt to understand and experience what the other person is going through.

Being an effective listener also demands that while the other person is talking we are not planning what we will say when he finishes. It requires acceptance, without prejudicial judgment, of what the person is saying and how he is saying it. Furthermore, it requires the ability to restate accurately both the content and the feeling of what has been communicated. Someone who gives his life to other people shows that he cares by really listening.

As we have seen with the other qualities of a strong Christian man, imparting your life to other people is not necessarily easy. But then, much of life is not easy. God is the source of all the power we need to be mature men. We must avoid selfishness and false strength, and instead tap into that divine power source. A true Christian does not shy away from the work of giving himself to other people.

ACTION STEPS

Go back to your evaluation on personal transparency earlier in the chapter. Reflect on your responses and what you can do to begin to cultivate such openness. Use the tips I gave you as a starter. Write your action steps below.

CHAPTER ELEVEN

Strength
in Servanthood

Becoming a Servant Leader

S everal months ago as I sat in a 747 flying cross-country, a lovely flight attendant graciously served me. Her pleasantness so impressed me that when she gave me my meal, I said to her, "Of all the great servants in the world, you have to be one of the best."

She pierced me with her eyes and said in a curt voice, "How dare you say that to me! I am no servant!" Then she stomped away.

Every time she served me after that she exhibited the same abrupt attitude. Finally, overtaken by curiosity to know what caused her to respond that way, I asked her.

She replied, "A servant is the worst thing anyone could ever call me."

I responded by saying, "I'm a Christian. The One I love most in the world is Jesus Christ, and Scripture says He was the greatest servant who ever lived. Therefore, when I say 'servant,' I mean someone great. That's the highest of compliments!"

My explanation didn't seem to change her mind, but it was important for me to explain what I meant. And she needed to hear it. Sometimes we Christians become so comfortable with our terminology that we forget certain words may have an entirely different connotation among nonbelievers. Maybe after she thought it over, she would accept my praise.

Nevertheless, her reaction showed me how misunderstood the term "servant" is in our society. In his book *Improving Your Serve,* Charles R. Swindoll describes his earliest concept of a servant:

> Washing around in my head was a caricature of a pathetic creature
> virtually without will or purpose in life…bent over, crushed in spirit,

lacking self-esteem, soiled, wrinkled, and weary. You know, sort of a human mule who, with a sigh, shuffles and trudges down the long rows of life.[1]

That misconception is probably more widely held than we can imagine, and is directly opposite of an accurate biblical view of a servant. What do you think? Think of the word "servanthood," and what picture comes to mind? Is it akin to what Chuck Swindoll thought, or is it different?

When I talk about servanthood in this chapter, I am talking about a picture totally different from the typical misinterpretation. I am talking about a key element of real manhood and effective leadership. I draw my conclusions from 1 Thessalonians 2:9, where Paul says,

> You recall, brethren, our labor and hardship, how working night and day so as not to be a burden to any of you, we proclaimed to you the gospel of God.

Paul and his coworkers clearly were living a productive lifestyle, not as weak individuals lacking purpose, but as servant/leaders to the ones they ministered to. These men modeled servanthood in two distinct ways: they had a humble attitude, and they gave of themselves sacrificially. Let's see what these qualities are all about.

A HUMBLE ATTITUDE

Paul says they worked night and day so they would not be a burden to any of the Thessalonians. What a picture of humility! Man, think about it! These men were apostles. They had every right to demand the support of the people based on their status alone. However, they realized God was in control, not them; and they put others first. They chose to defer to the people. They gave up their rights for the sake of others, out of love for the King of kings.

I think most people would agree that, while truly humble men are some of the most pleasant to be around and work with, they are also the hardest to find.

Benjamin Disraeli stated, "Talk to a man about himself and he will listen for hours."

An unknown author penned, "The smallest package we have ever seen is a man wrapped up in himself."

Elizabeth Chevalier, author of the bestselling novel *Driven Women,* wrote in a letter, "Have you ever heard the one about the novelist who met an old friend?

After they had talked for two hours, the novelist said, 'Now we've talked about me long enough—let's talk about you! What did you think of my last novel?'"

This kind of prideful self-centeredness is so typical in our day and age. It's called *narcissism,* from a figure in Greek mythology. In ancient Greece an extremely handsome young man named Narcissus was totally enamored with his own physical perfection. Whenever he came to a pool of clear water, he stopped, sometimes for hours, to admire his image.

One day he said to himself, "You are handsome, Narcissus! There's nobody so handsome in the whole world!" He stooped down to kiss his reflection, fell into the water, and drowned. Greek lore says the gods turned him into the beautiful flower we call by his name today.

On the other hand, most of us have a confused view of real humility. In his excellent book *You're Someone Special,*[2] Bruce Narramore provides a helpful framework for understanding true humility. With his kind permission, I have adapted some of the following guidelines from his ideas. Let's look at what true humility is not, and then at what it is.

What Humility Is Not

Humility Is Not Inferiority

Romans 12:3 tells us not to think more highly of ourselves than we ought to. This does not imply that we are to have an inferior view of ourselves. According to Scripture, we all are people of great worth. No one is inferior to anyone else—we are just different from one another, each unique in the way the master Designer created us.

Humility Is Not an Underestimation of Our Abilities

Describing himself, Paul writes, "Actually I should have been commended by you, for in no respect was I inferior to the most eminent apostles, even though I am a nobody" (2 Corinthians 12:11).

Paul has a realistic sense of his own capability. In 1 Corinthians 12, we read that God has given each of us unique gifts, abilities that are absolutely necessary for building up the body of Christ. You may think you are only a hand, a finger, or even a hangnail in the kingdom, but my friend, know this: You are God's man. You are critical to His work. If you don't do what God has called you to do, you will not only hinder His work, but your disobedience will leave you miserable and unfulfilled.

Therefore, you cannot underestimate your abilities, background, contacts, position, or any other asset, no matter how trivial it may seem. Since those things are given by God, they must be handled with great respect. You must be a good steward of these gifts as you strive to glorify God.

Humility Is Not Self-Hatred

Understanding that we are sinful does not mean we hate ourselves. In Psalm 139:13–16 we read how God made our physical form and our nonphysical substance, our personalities. How can we hate something God fashioned while we were still in our mother's womb? It is impossible if we believe that God is a loving, caring, sovereign, masterful God.

Humility Is Not Passivity

Think of the example of Jesus Christ, the most vibrant manifestation of humility in all of Scripture. He was the One who overturned the tables of the moneychangers and the benches of those selling doves and chased them out of the house of God (Matthew 21:12–13). He was bold, aggressive, and righteously angry at them. He certainly did not use a passive approach.

So, if humility is not a sense of inferiority, self-hatred, or passivity, what is it?

WHAT HUMILITY IS

Humility Is Staying Broken before God

Humility includes other nonaggressive qualities. Perhaps the most important is a willingness to be broken (repentant of pride, selfishness, and sin) and yielded to God.

Did you know that God wants us to be broken all of the time? He uses people with "a broken and contrite heart" (Psalm 51:17). He wants our spirits to be yielded to Him constantly so we can do His will and not just our own. That is the very essence of humility—staying yielded to God.

So what does such a life of brokenness look like?

- It means spending time daily with God because we know we need His power and insight.
- It means not demanding our own way even if we are right.
- It means leaning into God throughout the day—turning to Him for clarity, wisdom, sensitivity, and empowerment.
- It means maintaining a sweet, kind, gentle, transparent, and tender spirit before God and man.
- It means being teachable.

How teachable are you? Well, let's test this. How did you respond the last time you were criticized? Ouch! Hurt, didn't it? Think about it for a moment. What happened? How did you respond? How did you feel? What did you do? What did you say?

I remember some years ago when I was president of the International School of Theology with Campus Crusade for Christ. I was a young hotshot and enjoyed my position. One day a first-year student wanted to go out for lunch with me. During the meal he told me I was a great president and leader. So-o-o-o, I picked up the tab.

Then he said, "There are two more things I would like to talk to you about. May I?"

Well, I just imagined what he wanted to say: "Of all the great leaders in the world, you have to be one of them." So I said, "Sure, speak!"

And he did. But not what I'd hoped to hear. "I'm sure you're not aware of them, but there are two things in your life that I believe impede your walk with God and your effectiveness."

"Say, what?" He repeated his statement.

I blew up internally. I was so offended that I wanted to lash out. *Who does he think he is, this punk?* was my first thought.

As I leaned forward to give him the benefit of my wisdom, it seemed the hand of God grabbed me by the scruff of the neck and shook me a few times, and I heard these words: "Ron, why are you so surprised that someone sees something in your life that you need to deal with? Imagine if he saw everything *I* see."

Whoa! Good point! *How arrogant can I be that such a rebuke should offend me?* That became one of the defining moments in my life. It began a turn-around in how I responded to criticism.

Now, whenever someone points out a weakness in my life, here's how I respond: "That's nothing! You ought to know me the way God knows me. I am a lot worse than that!" It's so true!

Hey, don't react. Don't blow up as I almost did. It's true, you know: we are a lot worse than what anyone but God sees. So we may as well admit it. Then we will be much more willing to hear and comprehend what a brother or sister is taking a risk to tell us. If we can maintain an honest brokenness by God's grace, willing to confront our faults and even be rebuked and corrected when necessary, we will have the foundation of usability before God.

Humility Is Trusting God to Work through You and Your Gifts

We must stay broken and yielded to God on the one hand, and rest in the power of God to work through us on the other hand. This is nowhere better stated than in Philippians 4:13: "I can do all things through Him who strengthens me."

Notice what Paul says he can do: *all things*. Then how he can do them: *with strength that comes from Jesus*.

Paul doesn't say, "I am worthless and insignificant." Nor does he say, "I can do it all by myself." But remember, he began with brokenness. Based on that brokenness, he lived assertively, believing that the God of the universe had chosen him and would work mightily through him.

That is exactly how you and I are to live, as men and as leaders—humble but confident, broken but victorious, a servant and a leader, because we can do all things through Him who strengthens us. My friend, God has called you to be His, and to do great things through Him who strengthens you. Do you believe this? The world has to reckon with you and with the God in you. I encourage you to embrace that fact and live like the child of the King you are.

One day on another plane trip, I sat next to a distinguished-looking gentleman who turned to me and asked what I did. I was all dressed up, so I thought I'd try a new one.

"I'm an ambassador," I said.

"An ambassador? Of what country?"

"Oh, it's bigger than a country."

"What do you represent that's bigger than a country?"

I unpacked my ambassadorship. "I represent a kingdom, the biggest kingdom of all, the kingdom of God. You see, I am a kingdom rep. Wherever I go, I represent the King of kings, Jesus Christ, because I am a Christian and He has called me to be His ambassador. Are you part of that kingdom?" That led us into a great discussion.

You and I are "ambassadors for Christ" (2 Corinthians 5:20). The way we act, walk, dress, talk, think, and live must reflect that reality. This also means embracing and utilizing our gifts.

In Romans 12:6, Paul says we should exercise the various gifts each of us has been given. A truly humble person is one who knows his strengths and his weaknesses, who appreciates both and learns how to handle both.

For instance, I know I am a strong, motivating speaker. I'm creative, entrepreneurial, and a reasonably good leader. I also know that I do not like to give attention to details, to be involved in follow-through, or to impart myself to people in the way I should. I need to work on my weaknesses. I also need to focus on my strengths. Mostly, I need to be aware of them all and learn how to live my life in light of both my strengths and my weaknesses.

Do you truly believe you can "do everything" through the One who gives you strength? Do you live in brokenness with a pliable, sensitive, teachable spirit? Do you trust God to work through you in a mighty way as He answers prayer and empowers you to impact your world?

GIVING OURSELVES SACRIFICIALLY

Based on a spirit of humility, servanthood also manifests a life of sacrificial giving.

In 1 Thessalonians 2:9, Paul says that he, Timothy, and Silvanus worked "night and day." These men sacrificed. They gave of themselves. The concept of sacrificially giving ourselves to others is seen throughout Scripture. Just note these passages:

> For you were called to freedom, brethren; only do not turn your freedom into an opportunity for the flesh, but through love serve one another. (Galatians 5:13)

> And let us consider how to stimulate one another to love and good deeds. (Hebrews 10:24)

> Be devoted to one another in brotherly love; give preference to one another in honor; not lagging behind in diligence, fervent in spirit, serving the Lord; rejoicing in hope, persevering in tribulation, devoted to prayer, contributing to the needs of the saints, practicing hospitality. (Romans 12:10–13)

At the heart of these passages is an attitude of sacrificial giving of one's life, one's time, and one's finances. The classic passage on the giving of finances is 2 Corinthians 8. However, this passage has a great deal to do with giving in general. From this passage, note the first five verses below:

> Now, brethren, we wish to make known to you the grace of God which has been given in the churches of Macedonia, that in a great ordeal of affliction their abundance of joy and their deep poverty overflowed in the wealth of their liberality. For I testify that according to their ability, and beyond their ability they gave of their own accord, begging us with much entreaty for the favor of participation in the support of the saints, and this, not as we had expected, but they first gave themselves to the Lord and to us by the will of God. (2 Corinthians 8:1–5)

It is important to note the context of this particular passage. As Paul traveled through Europe, specifically in ancient Macedonia, he told of the need of fellow Christians in Jerusalem. The fact that the Macedonian region was suffering horrible economic depression adds to the impact of the whole story. As Chuck Swindoll points out, "Macedonia was to Paul a lot like India is to us. It would be like encouraging the people of Appalachia to respond to those who are hurting in the ghetto of Harlem."[3] Yet the Christians of Macedonia did respond and gave well beyond their ability.

There's a lot we can learn about sacrificial giving from the way these Christians gave of themselves. To give unselfishly, in the spirit of servanthood, we should:

Give Anonymously

No specific church is mentioned in this passage. We read simply, "the churches in Macedonia." They had no need to be noticed.

I often say, "I don't mind serving others so long as someone notices." Of course I am kidding—I think. It is not easy to serve others and not be noticed. But true servanthood needs no recognition. In fact, it seeks to not be recognized by anyone but God, who checks our inner motives.

A true servant's heart, then, is typified by anonymity.

Give Generously

When they gave, they "overflowed" in the process; they gave "beyond their ability." This type of sacrificial giving is typified by Onesiphorus, who modeled great generosity in his love for Paul:

> The Lord grant mercy to the house of Onesiphorus for he often refreshed me, and was not ashamed of my chains; but when he was in Rome, he eagerly searched for me, and found me—the Lord grant to him to find mercy from the Lord on that day—and you know very well what services he rendered at Ephesus. (2 Timothy 1:16–18)

Alexander Whyte, the preacher from Edinburgh, Scotland, wrote this in a biography of Onesiphorus:

> Paul might be the greatest of the apostles to Onesiphorus, and he may be all that and far more than all that to you and to me, but he was only Number so and so to the soldier who was chained night and day to Paul's right hand. You would not have known Paul from any con-

vict in our own penal settlements. Paul was simply "Number 5," or "Number 50," or "Number 500," or some such number. From one barrack-prison therefore to another Onesiphorus went about seeking for Paul day after day, week after week, often insulted, often threatened, often ill-used, often arrested and detained, till he was set free again only after great suffering and great expense. Till, at last, his arms were round Paul's neck, and the two old men were kissing one another and weeping to the amazement of all the prisoners who saw the scene. Noble-hearted Onesiphorus! We bow down before thee.[4]

My friend, how well does your life match up with that of Onesiphorus? He knew sacrificial giving. That is precisely the kind of giving God is calling us to do.

Give Voluntarily

The Living Bible translates 2 Corinthians 8:3–4 as: "I can testify that they did it because they wanted to and not because of nagging on my part. They begged us to take the money so they could share in the joy of helping." There is no joy in giving because one has to. Obligation is a terrible motivation for giving; it puts a damper on receiving too!

I just received a phone call from my older brother, Dick. He and his wife Jean lost their home and all of their possessions yesterday when a fire consumed their entire apartment complex. And they have no insurance. Dick, one of the greatest guys I know, responded with humility, hope, and a tremendous sense of perspective. "We'll just rebuild slowly and do what we need to do. We still have what counts—our lives."

As soon as I got off the phone with Dick, I had another call, from one of my associates. When I told her what had happened, her immediate response was deep compassion. She asked, "What can I do? Can I send money, clothes, utensils—what? Whatever they need, Ron, please let me know and count me in on helping them." She doesn't even know Dick and Jean. But she knows the Lord and has a generous, giving heart.

Frankly, I hadn't even thought about asking her for help. She volunteered. What about you? Do you give quickly, freely, voluntarily when someone is in need of your time, talents, or treasures?

Give Personally

You cannot give to others in an at-arm's-length manner. It involves time and effort and most likely you will need to adapt your schedule to fit others' needs.

Giving involves personal commitment.

Early one morning when my son was five, he and I decided to take a trip in the car. We had only about an hour to spend. I wanted to watch a softball game but Matt wanted to go to the park and play on the swings. I bought him a soda, thinking I could buy his allegiance to the game. However, when we got to the ball field, he kept saying he wanted to go to the park. I resisted until God cracked me over the head and said, "Ron, you are being utterly selfish. If you want to be a servant, a great servant, to your child and to Me, meet his needs. Flex your desires to his. Model to him what a godly father really is." So I surrendered my schedule and took him to the park, and we had a delightful time.

Again, bending my schedule for someone else is hard for me to do. How about you? That's the kind of personal giving God wants of us if we are to be the real men who are needed in this day and age—humble men, ready and willing to serve.

Action Steps

Identify one person in your life to serve this week. Write your answers to the following questions about how that serving will look. Go ahead, do it now!

1. How, when, and where will you give sacrificially?

2. How will you be anonymous, generous, voluntary, and personal in your giving?

3. What role will the use of your gifts play?

4. How will your humble attitude show?

5. How will God be working supernaturally through you?

CHAPTER TWELVE

WORKING HARD

Being God's Man of Steel

Have you ever met a prima donna in the workplace? Someone whose position in the hierarchy is so important to him he won't do anything he considers beneath his status?

A man was recently promoted to an executive position by the company president. The promotion did a great deal for his sagging self-image; in fact, too much. He spends nearly all his evenings at the office and refuses to help his wife with household jobs they had previously enjoyed doing together. Saturdays had been family days; now the children cry as their daddy leaves the house Saturday mornings for golf with other company executives.

One day, just before leaving for work, the man paused at a mirror for a glimpse of himself, smartly dressed for success, and said to his wife, "Honey, how many really great men do you think there are in this country?"

"I don't know," she replied, "but I'd guess there is one less than you think!"

Prima donnas are never very popular, at least not as popular as they think they are. We all probably know at least one such person. You know the type. They delegate nearly all their work, not because they are too busy, but because they consider themselves too valuable to be wasted on certain tasks. Or they are just lazy.

Frankly, the body of Christ today is filled with far too many people like this. There is far too little steel in the veins of the average Christian man.

How about you? Are you rigorous in your work habits? Or do you find yourself soft, lazy, maybe even wimpy here? Do challenges overwhelm you or do they motivate you to move ahead? Do problems easily discourage you or have you cultivated the art of finishing well?

Paul, Timothy, and Silvanus could never be described as prima donnas. As you know, Paul writes in verse 9 of 1 Thessalonians 2 that he and his coworkers were involved in hard labor. The word labor in the Greek is *kopos,* meaning hard, worrisome toil that causes fatigue. They worked night and day at the tent-making trade to make money to help fulfill the needs of the

Thessalonians. Paul could have demanded his rights as an apostle and asked for money, but he did not assert his authority—he worked hard as a result of his love for the people he served.

OTHER HARD WORKERS

Hard, noncomplaining work has always been a key to success.

Theodore Roosevelt said, "I am only an average man, but I work harder at it than the average man." This commitment to hard work is illustrated in the lives of great men throughout history.

The United States Patent Office granted Thomas Edison 1098 patents, 122 of them before he was thirty years of age! Edison's comment on his seventy-fifth birthday is worth noting: "Work heals and ennobles."

Martin Luther preached almost daily; he lectured constantly as a professor; he was burdened with the direction of all the churches in his denomination; controversies perpetually harassed him, and he was one of the most voluminous writers of his day—his correspondence fills many volumes.

While in Strasbourg, John Calvin preached or lectured every day. In Geneva, he was pastor, professor, and almost magistrate. He lectured every other day; he preached daily; he was overwhelmed with letters from all parts of Europe; he authored works so numerous that they would seem more than enough to occupy his whole time; and all this in the midst of infirmity of the flesh.

John Wesley averaged three sermons a day for fifty-four years, preaching, all told, more than 44,000 times. In doing this, he traveled by horseback and carriage more than 200,000 miles, or about 5,000 miles a year. His published works include a four-volume commentary on the entire Bible; a dictionary of the English language; a five-volume work on natural philosophy; a four-volume work on church history; histories of England and Rome; grammars on the Hebrew, Latin, Greek, French, and English languages; three works on medicine; six volumes of church music; and seven volumes of sermons and controversial papers.

He also edited a library of fifty volumes known as *The Christian Library*. He was greatly devoted to pastoral work. Later, Wesley had the additional burden of supervising all the churches in his movement. He arose at 4 A.M. and worked solidly through to 10 P.M., allowing brief periods for meals.

In the midst of all this work he declared, "I have more hours of private retirement than any man in England." At age eighty-three, he was piqued to discover that he could not write any more than fifteen hours a day without hurting his eyes; and at the age of eighty-six he was ashamed to admit that he could not preach more than twice a day. In his eighty-sixth year, he preached in almost every shire in England and Wales and often rode thirty to fifty miles a day.

Only a few decades ago, a man's willingness to work hard was the only reference necessary to secure a job. Today, generally speaking, we have become relatively lazy. We desire shorter working days, more vacation time, and someone to whom we can delegate unwanted responsibilities. We do not seek to be diligent, but rather to be creative with the time we spend on our jobs. But a real man, a true leader, is not afraid of hard work; he admires that quality and seeks to cultivate it in himself.

A New Perspective

In this chapter I want to share some core competencies that may give us a fresh perspective on hard work. If we can internalize these concepts and use them, we will not fear a rigorous lifestyle—in fact, we'll thrive on it!

1. Expect life to be tough!
2. Remember whom you serve.
3. Focus on the roots of your life.
4. Renew yourself daily.

1. Expect Life to Be Tough

I tried to think of a more pleasant description of this aspect of being a godly leader, but I could find no better word than "pain." Paul was involved in labor and hardship. The word "hardship" is the same term translated "labors" in 2 Corinthians 6:5. Note the conditions surrounding it: "in beatings, in imprisonments, in tumults, in labors, in sleeplessness, in hunger."

This term is also used in 2 Corinthians 11:23 where we read: "in far more labors, in far more imprisonments, beaten times without number, often in danger of death." Paul, Timothy, and Silvanus were involved in great pain, a natural by-product of being a leader.

We must embrace the fact that life is tough. In fact, the more committed to Christ we become, the greater stress we will experience. Isn't that fun?

Let me explain the term. By "stress" I mean pressure, difficulties, and tensions. I do not mean worry, fear, anger, or depression. Whenever you are faced with a challenge, you can respond distressfully (the unbiblical way) or eustress-fully (the biblical way). Eustress is when you turn your problem into a possi-bility, when it motivates you to meet the challenge. This causes you to grow, and, in fact, become empowered.

This is exactly the way Paul and his partners responded to the situations they encountered. So, though their stresses increased, their internal growth and power also increased. The more they grew, the more empowered and committed they became—and that created more stress. Also, the more they lived on the edge spiritually, the more satanic warfare they experienced. Satan sought to get them off track as he will seek to do with us. That only added to their stress!

In 2 Corinthians 4:5 Paul states, "We do not preach ourselves but Christ Jesus as Lord, and ourselves as your bond-servants for Jesus' sake." A few verses later he adds, "We are afflicted in every way, but not crushed; perplexed, but not despairing; persecuted, but not forsaken; struck down, but not destroyed" (4:8–9).

Notice the kind of strain Paul refers to here. He uses four key terms to explain: afflicted, perplexed, persecuted, and struck down. Have you ever felt like that? I sure have. In fact, Paul said it was their way of life. Let's look at these terms one at a time.

Affliction

The Greek word for affliction indicates intense pressure. This could have been brought on by difficult circumstances or antagonistic people. The word could be translated, "to treat with hostility." This affliction is typified in 2 Corinthians 11:27–28:

> I have been in labor and hardship, through many sleepless nights, and hunger and thirst, often without food, in cold and exposure. Apart from such external things, there is the daily pressure upon me of con-cern for all the churches.

Talk about pressure!

In recent years there has been much research on stress, its causes and results. One major piece measures the stress factor of typical afflictions in life-changing units.[1] The greater the number of units you experience, the greater the risk of emotional or physical illness in the ensuing months. For example, if you endure 200 to 299 units in a given year, your probability of suffering ill-ness within the next two years is 50 percent. If it is 300 or more units, your chance jumps to 80 percent. Here is a list of some of the pressure situations and their corresponding life-changing units:

Death of spouse	100
Divorce	73
Marital separation from mate	65
Detention in jail or other institution	63
Death of a close family friend	63
Major personal injury or illness *Annie*	53
Marriage	50
Being fired at work	47
Marital reconciliation with mate	45
Retirement from work	45
Major change in the health or behavior of a family member	44
Pregnancy	40
Sexual difficulties	39
Gaining a new family member (through birth, adoption, oldster moving in, etc.)	39
Major change in financial state (a lot worse off or a lot better off than usual)	38
Death of a close friend	37
Son or daughter leaving home (marriage, attending college, etc.)	29
In-law troubles	29
Troubles with the boss	23
Major change in working hours or conditions	20
Changing residence	20
Changing to a new school	20
Vacation	13
Christmas	12
Minor violations of the law (traffic tickets, disturbing the peace, etc.)	11

Paul's life-changing pressure units must have been several hundred! Yet he said that, though he was afflicted (stressed), he was not crushed (distressed). Why?

Paul had learned to accept life as difficult and, as we will see shortly, he maintained the right perspective on issues. We must do the same. Remember, the problem with the above-mentioned life-change unit research is that it is based on the assumption that man always reflects his environment. But this does not necessarily need to happen with us! As Christian men, we are not to be conformed to the world (reflecting our environment), but to be transformed by the renewing of our minds (which results in actually transforming our environment). Put another way, we are not thermometers (reflecting the temperature), but thermostats (*determining* the temperature). There is a radical difference, right?

Perplexity

The Greek term for *perplexed* means 'without a way'. The perplexed individual does not know where or to whom to turn for help. He does not have the necessary resources to handle a given situation and is at a loss as to what direction to take.

Paul must have felt this way often during his times of mistreatment and imprisonment. In 2 Corinthians 11:26 we read:

> I have been on frequent journeys, in dangers from rivers, dangers from robbers, dangers from my countrymen, dangers from the Gentiles, dangers in the city, dangers in the wilderness, dangers on the sea, dangers among false brethren.

Imagine! Eight times in this one verse, Paul uses the word *danger!*

If you feel bewildered or frustrated or confused, accept it. It's part of being a man. Paul experienced it. We cannot deny the reality of the confusion that surrounds manhood.

Persecution

Originally the term *persecute* meant 'to run after, to pursue'. It is an aggressive word conveying everything from being "chased" by intimidation to being outright assaulted. Persecution is a natural result of the desire to follow Christ.

In fact, Scripture makes a promise that most people do not care to claim: "All who desire to live godly in Christ Jesus will be persecuted" (2 Timothy 3:12). Such persecution is reflected upon by the apostle Paul:

Five times I received from the Jews thirty-nine lashes. Three times I was beaten with rods, once I was stoned, three times I was shipwrecked, a night and a day I have spent in the deep. (2 Corinthians 11:24–25)

Can you imagine the abuse Paul suffered?

In addition to the physical abuse a servant may experience is the emotional abuse people often endure. A classic example of this is Daniel. He was faithful, diligent, honest, he served others with a pure heart.

However, he ran into problems. The very people he loved and worked for turned on him. They sought to disprove his integrity. Can you imagine how Daniel felt?

Then this Daniel began distinguishing himself among the commissioners and satraps because he possessed an extraordinary spirit, and the king planned to appoint him over the entire kingdom. Then the commissioners and satraps began trying to find a ground of accusation against Daniel in regard to government affairs; but they could find no ground of accusation or evidence of corruption, inasmuch as he was faithful, and no negligence or corruption was to be found in him. (Daniel 6:3–4)

Evil men began attacking his character, spreading innuendos about him. His words, his actions, his motives—all were brought under suspicion. That's persecution!

Struck Down

When Paul says they were struck down, the idea is: being thrown down, shoved aside, or rejected. This explains why J. B. Phillips paraphrases this as "we may be knocked down." Being knocked down can be painfully embarrassing.

I remember vividly my days of Pee Wee Football. When I was ten I had two years of Pee Wee Football eligibility left, but I weighed too much. I finally lost the necessary twenty pounds to make the 104-pound weight limit. On our team we had an A-string, a B-string, a C-string, a D-string, and a D-2 string. I played on the D-2. Since I was an offensive lineman, I had the dream that every lineman has, that I'd get the ball and run with it like all those running backs and ends who always get the glory.

I'm not sure what happened during that fateful game, but somehow a ball got loose and ended up in my arms. There I was with the ball! I was so thrilled that I took off running. This was my day of glory. I could just see my name in the local newspaper. I am not sure how far I ran (probably about six yards), but I was quickly knocked down. It was so humiliating. The only way I could handle being knocked down was remembering that I had actually picked up the ball and run with it. I was shocked when I realized that the one who knocked me down was my own teammate. Furthermore, the reason he knocked me down was that I was running the wrong way.

"Struck down" in our Scripture context was much more serious than a football game. It meant mortal danger. Note Paul's statements:

- Shipwrecked three times (11:25).
- A day and a night spent in the ocean (11:25).
- Surrounded by constant dangers (11:26).
- Without sufficient food (11:27).
- Exposed to the elements (11:27).
- Escaping death by being let down a wall in a large basket (11:33).

Remember, Paul was innocent of any wrongdoing. How unfair for him to be treated this way. Yet the beauty of the record of these four stresses he encountered—affliction, perplexity, persecution, and rejection—is Paul's attitude through all of it. Notice his perspective in the following verses:

> Always carrying about in the body the dying of Jesus, that the life of Jesus also may be manifested in our body. For we who live are constantly being delivered over to death for Jesus' sake, that the life of Jesus also may be manifested in our mortal flesh....
> Therefore we do not lose heart, but though our outer man is decaying, yet our inner man is being renewed day by day. For momentary, light affliction is producing for us an eternal weight of glory far beyond all comparison, while we look not at the things which are seen, but at the things which are not seen; for the things which are seen are temporal, but the things which are not seen are eternal. (2 Corinthians 4:10–11, 16–18)

This servant/leader looked not at things seen, but at things unseen. He focused on eternity. He knew God would make all things right. Paul's stress resulted in eustress, not distress, as his inner man was being renewed day by day.

Wow! That is a true servant of God. He endured the pain joyfully because he had a right perspective on God, himself, and other people. He had accepted the fact that life was tough and the work was hard.

2. Remember Whom You Serve

Beyond embracing the toughness of life (the foundation of hard work), we must remember whom we serve. Ephesians 6:6 says it well:

> Obey them not only to win their favor when their eye is on you, but like slaves of Christ, doing the will of God from your heart. Serve wholeheartedly, as if you were serving the Lord, not men, because you know that the Lord will reward everyone for whatever good he does, whether he is slave or free. (NIV)

Do you get the point? You and I are to serve our Lord Jesus Christ all of the time. Whether at work or in ministry, our ultimate mission is not to serve man, but Christ. Serving Him is to be our purpose, our motivation, and our way of life.

Therefore, we need to work diligently. Get engaged. Make a difference. Our standard is nothing short of excellence, because we serve the King.

3. Focus on the Roots of Your Life

A third core competency needed for hard work is that of a right focus. Too often we get enamored with the "fruit," or results, of our work—material success, position, happiness, numbers. And in doing so, we not only miss the boat, we miss the blessing. Let me suggest a radical thought: Forget these.

Oh, it's okay to stop periodically and enjoy the fruits of your labors. But if you focus on them, make them your purpose and goals, you will lose your perspective. Remember, God produces the fruit! That is His job. And His fruit is love, joy, peace, patience, kindness, goodness, faithfulness, gentleness, and self-control.

Rather than focusing on the world's "fruits," we instead should focus on the "roots" to a successful life, on doing what God says. And God says to walk in the Spirit, live in obedience, meditate on the Word, discipline ourselves for godliness, and pray without ceasing, among other disciplines. Our job is to do these things. God will bless us for doing them. Now, He may not bless us the way we necessarily want, or according to our timetable, but don't worry—His blessings will be beyond measure.

My friend Ken Blanchard, coauthor of *One-Minute Manager*, says we often live life like the tennis player who spends all of his time watching the scoreboard (fruit). He will never win until he starts to focus on the ball (the roots).

We must do the same thing, my friend!

Ask yourself where your focus is. Are you focusing more on the fruit in your life or the roots? How can you change? Do it!

4. Renew Yourself Daily

It is one thing to work hard, but another to burn out. As I speak about hard work, I don't want to feed a harmful addiction you might have, workaholism. Frankly, that is a danger today. And it may be one for you.

Watch out! People in business often burn themselves out, and so can people in ministry. We should work hard. That's made abundantly clear to us. There will be pressures. That is obvious. And it won't be easy. Get used to it.

But remember this: God wants you to be a useful vessel in His hands. Therefore, we must refresh ourselves daily. We must care for the vessel mentally, emotionally, physically, spiritually, and relationally.

Dr. Richard Swenson wrote a very helpful book along these lines some time ago titled *Margins.* His thesis is that just as a page of a book needs margins to save us from eye strain, so you and I need margins in every area of our lives to save us from life strain. We get this white space by intentionally, proactively cultivating it.

This means we give deliberate attention to each area of our lives and construct the appropriate margins.

If your bank account is drying up, build a financial margin by either spending less or earning more.

If you're getting tired and sluggish, check your physical margin. Get a checkup. Get a little more sleep; improve your eating habits; get better, regular exercise.

If you sense a spiritual dryness, identify whether the issue is some specific sin of commission or omission, a lack of time with the Lord, or some other devotional problem. Then take action to deal with the specific need and rebuild your margin.

The best way to prevent burnout is to not wait until the problem occurs. Instead, build those margins into your life as you go along. Look at the vital areas of your life on a weekly basis and then ask yourself two questions: Where was past neglect? Where is present need? Based on your answers, set your week's priorities and then build these margins into your schedule.

Think of a lumberman who goes out to cut down several trees. He doesn't just cut and cut with the same ax and never stop to sharpen it. Instead, he sharpens his ax on a routine basis, at a scheduled time, so he can get more cutting done more effectively. He knows his margins and his priorities.

I have learned over the years that if I am to be effective I must establish and maintain those margins. For example, during my day it's often difficult to find quiet time for studying, preparing a talk, or writing. So I get margin by going to bed early (9 P.M. or so) and getting up early (about 4 A.M.). I lose certain social benefits at night, but I gain great productivity in the morning. In fact, I began this morning at 4:15 (I slept in) and wrote much of this chapter before the rest of my time zone awakened.

That works for me. What works for you? Think about this carefully and begin the art of building margins into your life to renew yourself daily.

How we need men with a genuine, healthy work commitment today! Men of steel! Imagine what the working world, our government, our educational system, and our churches would be like if we had more real men who are not afraid of hard labor. Instead of having a society in which men fight for their own rights, we would see men pulling together, sacrificing for each other.

But a dream of what society could be never answers the need of the moment. We need concerned, committed leaders *today.* We can't wait for others to become this type of leader; we must step out and begin to lead others in this way ourselves.

Action Steps

Look again at the four core competencies discussed in this chapter. Rate yourself on the scale below on each item (2 = weak; 8 = strong).

1. Expect life to be tough!	2 4 6 8
2. Remember whom you serve.	2 4 6 8
3. Focus on the roots of your life.	2 4 6 8
4. Keep renewing yourself daily.	2 4 6 8

Circle the one in which you rated yourself the weakest. Take a few minutes and write out an action plan of what you can do this week to grow in this area.

CHAPTER THIRTEEN

A WINNING LIFESTYLE

Not Perfect but Progressing

Your life speaks so loudly I can't hear what you say."

"Do as I say, not as I do."

I'm sure you've heard those statements before. They touch on the concept of having our walk match our talk and our life match our lips. If I am speaking one thing and living another, people see nothing but contradiction and hypocrisy.

I recently heard about a man who met regularly with some other friends in a small group to discuss their opinions on various issues. On one particular day, the conversation went along well until the first individual became agitated. He not only attacked the problem but he also attacked the individual who was taking a viewpoint contrary to his. He didn't realize that he was offensive, but from that point on nobody heard anything he said. His actions spoke so loudly that his words, though probably accurate, were discounted.

A mature Christian man realizes that he is an example, even if not by choice. "You are witnesses, and so is God, of how holy, righteous and blameless we were among you who believed" (1 Thessalonians 2:10, NIV).

Let's look at being an example and the power that comes with it, at a pattern we can model, and at the net product or qualities we are to exemplify.

BEING AN EXAMPLE: THE POWER

We are strong examples to each other, whether good or bad, and sometimes that brings out some nervous humor.

"The new washerwoman has stolen two of our towels—the crook!" exclaimed the wife.

"Which towels, dear?" her husband asked.

"You know, the ones we took from the hotel in Miami Beach."

Paul, Timothy, and Silvanus, three mature Christian men, understood the negative and positive power of example. Scripture has some powerful things to say about avoiding bad examples:

> When you enter the land which the LORD your God gives you, you shall not learn to imitate the detestable things of those nations. (Deuteronomy 18:9)

> Do not associate with a man given to anger; or go with a hot-tempered man, lest you learn his ways, and find a snare for yourself. (Proverbs 22:24–25)

> You therefore, beloved, knowing this beforehand, be on your guard lest, being carried away by the error of unprincipled men, you fall from your own steadfastness. (2 Peter 3:17)

The wrong kind of company can be a strong negative influence on our lives. Scripture tells us to stay away from those people who will affect us in the wrong way. Scripture also encourages us to be good examples:

> Not because we do not have the right to this, but in order to offer ourselves as a model for you, that you might follow our example. (2 Thessalonians 3:9)

> Let no one look down on your youthfulness, but rather in speech, conduct, love, faith and purity, show yourself an example of those who believe. (1 Timothy 4:12)

> In all things show yourself to be an example of good deeds. (Titus 2:7)

Now let's look more specifically at what the apostle Paul says about following his example:

> I exhort you therefore, be imitators of me. (1 Corinthians 4:16)

> Be imitators of me, just as I also am of Christ. (1 Corinthians 11:1)

Brethren, join in following my example, and observe those who walk according to the pattern you have in us. (Philippians 3:17)

The things you have learned and received and heard and seen in me, practice these things; and the God of peace shall be with you. (Philippians 4:9)

Can you imagine telling other people to copy you? Can you imagine promising them peace if they do?

Why did Paul make these strong statements? He knew the power of example. He was ministering to a group of new Christians who desperately needed a picture of what the Christian life ought to be. Paul knew that they would ultimately become like the people around them, especially their leaders. Therefore, Paul insisted that Christians, especially those in leadership positions, set godly standards and live by them.

Whether we like it or not, we are witnesses for Christ, a model for others to emulate. The reality of this is not in question. The question is: What kind of witnesses or models are we?

As in Paul's day, people around us are watching and will consciously or unconsciously emulate our behavior. What will the results be?

This was driven home to me when my son Matt was small. He was just tall enough to stand on a stool and begin to go to the bathroom by himself. I carefully watched him as he unzipped his little shorts and then, before relieving himself, spat into the toilet.

"Why did you do that?" I asked.

"Because you always spit, Dad," he responded. And you know what? He was absolutely right. I picked up this habit years ago. I guess Matt thought it was the way to prime the pump or something. In any case, he emulated me.

What are your children copying from you? What about your friends? Your coworkers? Are they picking up bad attitudes and habits or good attitudes and habits?

What legacy are you leaving through your lifestyle?

BEING AN EXAMPLE: THE PATTERN

Paul says that he, Timothy, and Silvanus were witnesses to the Thessalonians by living devoutly, uprightly, and blamelessly. A closer look at each of these concepts will give us a better understanding of the example these men set.

Devout

Devout could be translated, 'dedicated to the service of God.' Some translate it 'in holiness.' This kind of wholehearted dedication is seen in the resolves of famed early-American preacher Jonathan Edwards:

- Resolved, to live with all my might while I do live.
- Resolved, never to lose one moment of time, to improve it in the most profitable way.
- Resolved, never to do anything which I should despise or think meanly of in another.
- Resolved, never to do anything out of revenge.
- Resolved, never to do anything which I should be afraid to do if it were the last hour of my life.[1]

Such men as Edwards are wholly dedicated to the service of God out of tremendous reverence and obedience to Him. But note also, as in the example of Paul, how true devotion is a springboard to active resolve.

Upright

Upright is translated by some scholars as 'just' or 'righteous,' and this standard refers to conformity to God's design for living. It also implies integrity. A person who lives uprightly acts on the basis of principle rather than whim. This is typified by the life and sayings of President Abraham Lincoln.

> Lincoln showed the quality of this courage when, against the advice of Congress, he made the call for an additional 500,000 recruits. He was told it would prevent his re-election. With flashing in his eye, he replied: "It is not necessary for me to be re-elected, but it is necessary for the soldiers at the front to be reinforced by 500,000 men, and I shall call for them; and if I go down under the act, I will go down, like the Cumberland, with my colors flying.[2]

This type of integrity was also characteristic of Thomas Edison.

Edison once developed a talking doll—the only one of its kind then. The doll had a phonograph inside its body with prerecorded nursery rhymes. Several hundreds of the dolls were made before Edison knew that the right to manufacture phonograph toys had been sold by his company to another firm years before. Although this other firm never exercised the right, Edison stopped production of the talking dolls, and had the remaining ones destroyed. Only two are believed to be extant today.[3]

If you were asked to name a person who does something because it is just and correct, even if it means cost or sacrifice to him, who would come to your mind? I think of the professional golfer who needed only one putt to win a recent major tournament. But when he lined up for his putt he accidentally touched the ball, just barely. No one saw it and it was only an oh-so-slight tap. But according to the rules, even that slight touch counted as a stroke. So instead of burying it, he told the referee and lost the match.

I also think of the three-star general I met with yesterday. He is one of the top leaders in a major branch of the military. We were discussing how my organization, Future Achievement International, might help his branch of the military in the area of leadership development. I was taken by his commitment to help his people internalize the concept of doing the right thing, not because they were ordered to but because it was the right thing to do. His passion for integrity stunned me.

Lord, may his tribe increase. We need real men who do what's right and just in their personal lives, family relationships, business dealings, and ministry activity.

Are you such a man? If not, do you have the courage to become one?

Blameless

The final word Paul used in this triad is *blamelessly.* Paul was saying in essence that there was no basis for reproach by God or man in the relationships these individuals had with the Thessalonians. Paul did not say they were perfect—he simply claimed that their efforts to seek the good of the Thessalonians were so sincere that no reproach could be brought against them. These men sought to behave appropriately before God.

An unknown writer once penned, "The measure of man's real character is what he would do if he knew he would never be found out." The point for Christian men ought to be clear and penetrating: We must live blamelessly in our relationships with other people, and we must realize that God and man are our witnesses.

Now think about that for a minute. We are to be blameless not just before man but before God as well. Whoa! That is serious. God sees everything. He knows every motive we have—our thoughts, attitudes, and feelings.

Does that make you nervous? It should. That is part of what the "fear of

God" is about. God knows us inside and out, and holds us accountable for our actions and our words. You and I must embrace Solomon's admonition to "fear God and keep His commandments." We will reap what we sow. It does matter how we behave. Our actions do have consequences.

Am I grabbing your attention? God sees and He knows.

What would happen inside you if you received a letter that said simply, "I've been following you for months, and I know your secret"? Would you dismiss it as having no validity? Or would it cause panic because there is something in your life you'd rather keep hidden?

So often today, we men focus on how we come across outwardly—we become people-pleasers—while internally we stop growing. In fact, we become subtle con artists. We project one thing but when we are all alone we are something else altogether. We know inside that there is little power, joy, impact, or core godliness; in fact, there may be just the opposite.

When you look at your inner life, do you see honesty and growth, or are you trapped in phoniness and stagnation? Are you struggling with improper motivations, impure thoughts, unhealthy obsessions?

Realize that God knows. That is the bad news, and there's no hiding it. It is also the good news—God knows, but He loves you regardless!

Your way to freedom and growth can be summed up with the words "Walk in the light." If you will expose your sinfulness to the light (God's Word and His Spirit), turn from such sin, and rely upon the power of God's Spirit within you, you will be freed to live blamelessly.

You see, living blamelessly is not being perfect. Rather, it is staying in the light—admitting sin (frequently, if you are like me), embracing God's full forgiveness, and living with humility and boldness—a freed, totally loved, empowered man of God.

You may be filled with shame at this very moment over sins you have committed in the past and/or sin habits that plague you now. I understand. I have faced and still face my own demons. We all deal with the ever-present reality of sin around us and in us. But there is freedom. Let me illustrate.

Imagine a husband kissing his wife and children good-bye in the morning and then running out to hop into the car. It is a drizzly day and the ground is covered with mud puddles. In his haste, he slips in the mud and falls directly into a puddle. What does he do? He gets up, cleans himself off quickly, and rushes to work.

A little later in the day, his five-year-old son runs outside and looks for "Daddy's mud puddle" to jump into and play in.

It is one thing to slip in the mud puddle, get up and clean yourself off and move on; it is quite another to live in sin—to look for and play in the mud puddle (intentional, perpetual disobedience).

You will sin! You will blow it! Now, understand me. God wants you not to sin. He tells us in 1 John 2:1, "My little children, I am writing these things to you that you may not sin." God wants your utter purity.

But knowing the baggage we bring with us, John goes on to say, "And if anyone sins, we have an Advocate with the Father, Jesus Christ the righteous; and He Himself is the propitiation for our sins; and not for ours only, but also for those of the whole world."

You see, God wants you to be liberated. The way He does it is to have you become so overwhelmingly connected to His forgiveness of your sins that you respond in humble thankfulness and utter obedience—not because you must, but because of your deep appreciation of His love and grace.

So embrace your forgiveness. That's where it starts. You were forgiven at the cross. "As far as the east is from the west, so far has He removed our transgressions from us," says Psalm 103:12. In Jeremiah 31:34 the Lord says, "'I will forgive their iniquity, and their sin I will remember no more.'" Do you get the point? You are forgiven.

Let me ask you this: what color is sin? I asked that question to an audience of about 1500 last weekend at a marriage conference. Many said black. In fact, that is the typical answer. I guess it reflects the old cowboy movies—black hats and white hats. Actually, the answer is red.

Isaiah 1:18 says, "Though your sins are as scarlet, they will be as white as snow; though they are red like crimson, they will be like wool."

Have you ever been to a chicken ranch? Chickens will peck another chicken to death when they see the blood from a rupture caused by the laying of an egg. To deal with this, chicken ranchers use red cellophane or red paint on the windows to filter the light so the chickens don't see the blood. The blood is still there but it is invisible to the other chickens.

That, my friend, is what has happened to you and me. Our sin tests us during our entire lives but God sees us as holy because He sees us through the blood of Christ. Our sins have been filtered out. Not only have they been made invisible; they have also been thrown away.

So cast off your shame. Make right what you need to with God and others by confessing your sin—then move on. God wants to use you. He has designed you for His purposes. Don't let Satan sidetrack you with sin or guilt.

Meditate on this Scripture right now: "If we confess our sins, He is faithful and righteous to forgive us our sins and to cleanse us from all unrighteousness" (1 John 1:9).

Here is an effective step you can take at this moment. Pull out a sheet of paper and write down every sin you can think of that you have not confessed and for which you have not experienced God's forgiveness. Please take the time to do this. The first time I did, I thought I'd have four or five to list, but I filled the front and the back of an entire sheet of 8½-by-11-inch paper. Once these are written out, write the above Scripture across the top of the sheet, claim God's total forgiveness, and rip up and destroy the paper. You are forgiven!

Join me on this road of freedom in Christ.

BEING AN EXAMPLE: THE PRODUCT

What did Paul and his companions' devout, upright, and blameless lifestyle look like? I think the qualities in 1 Thessalonians 2 that we've studied in this book accurately describe their way of life.

Paul referred to these qualities in another way in Colossians 3:5–17. As we've noticed before, here he says we are to "put off the old man" (old manner of living) and "put on the new man" (new, Spirit-filled way of living).

> Therefore consider the members of your earthly body as dead to immorality, impurity, passion, evil desire, and greed, which amounts to idolatry....
>
> But now you also, put them all aside: anger, wrath, malice, slander, and abusive speech from your mouth. Do not lie to one another, since you laid aside the old self with its evil practices, and have put on the new self who is being renewed to a true knowledge according to the image of the One who created him....
>
> And so, as those who have been chosen of God, holy and beloved, put on a heart of compassion, kindness, humility, gentleness and patience; bearing with one another, and forgiving each other, whoever has a complaint against anyone; just as the Lord forgave you, so also should you. And beyond all these things put on love, which is the perfect bond of unity. And let the peace of Christ rule in your hearts, to which indeed you were called in one body; and be thankful. (Colossians 3:5, 8–10, 12–15)

You must deliberately cast off the old patterns and replace them with the new. This is a matter of "disciplining yourself for godliness" as we discussed in an earlier chapter. If you will do this in the power of the Holy Spirit, you will soon see the product. New and exciting patterns of godliness will begin to emerge.

TRAIT TO PUT OFF	DESCRIPTION
immorality	illicit sexual intercourse
impurity	inappropriate thoughts
passion	degrading emotions
evil desire	all manner of corrupt hopes
greed/idolatry	compelling desire for more; self-seeking
anger	slow burning anger, bitterness
wrath	quick-tempered outburst
malice	intentional, cruel meanness
slander	insulting speech to cause harm
abusive speech	foul mouthed; shameful speaking
lying	falsehood in any form

TRAIT TO PUT ON	DESCRIPTION
heart of compassion	selfless caring based on real empathy
kindness	treating everyone as important by honoring them
humility	submitting to God and putting His interests first
gentleness	tenderness based on real strength under control
patience	sustaining tough times joyfully
forbearance	enduring misuse by others and making allowances
forgiveness	overlooking and dropping others' offenses
love	deliberate demonstration of caring
peace	resting joyfully in the center of God's will
thankfulness	appreciation for God's goodness

Study these traits and descriptions and then meditate on the Colossians 3 Scripture quoted above.

Remember, the key here is to focus on the roots of putting off negative traits and putting on positive ones through godly discipline. Practice putting these traits off and on at least four times a day for several weeks. Depend upon the Spirit of God to give you wisdom, insight, and power. He'll produce the fruit. You focus on the roots.

These are the qualities that exemplify a Christian man living for Christ in a skeptical world. As you put them on habitually, just watch the power of your impact! Your compelling life will attract others who will want what you have. You will come to exemplify the steadfast holiness to which God calls Christian men.

Well, how are you feeling, my friend? Does this seem doable, or is it overwhelming? Remember, God has called you. He deeply desires to use you profoundly. With His help, you *can* live and model a winning lifestyle!

These lines of a poem by Henry Wadsworth Longfellow so well describe the long-term impact of our modeling. I invite you to reflect on the words.

FOOTPRINTS ON THE SAND

Lives of great men all remind us
We can make our lives sublime,
And, departing, leave behind us
Footprints on the sands of time.

Footprints, that perhaps another,
Sailing o'er life's solemn main,
A forlorn and shipwrecked brother
Seeing, shall take heart again.

—HENRY WADSWORTH LONGFELLOW

ACTION STEPS

Go back to the 1 John 1:9 passage mentioned earlier. Memorize it. That's right, memorize it! I know it may seem tough, but do it. You are God's man—a tough, committed, serious, godly Christian. Act like it. Scripture memorization is going to be a key factor in your growth. Meditate (think about, mull over and dwell on) that text at least four times a day for the next week.

Whenever you sin, apply the text, and believe it. This will build a new habit of responding biblically to your sin; it also will empower you to stop the sin and live in freedom.

CHAPTER FOURTEEN

Tough Love, Tender Love

The Art of Caring Confrontation

or the past hour your spouse has been treating you less than warmly. You feel you have done nothing wrong, but maybe you have been careless or inconsiderate, so you ask, "What's wrong, honey?"

"Nothing!"

The ice on that word could freeze boiling water. Her word said there was nothing wrong, but her tone of voice shouted that almost nothing was right.

How many times has that little scenario played itself out in your home—or with someone at your workplace? I'll bet you've even given that answer yourself a time or two. We all try to avoid something we find difficult—confrontation.

Why is it so hard to confront someone? If you think back to times you have been in situations like the one above, you'll probably realize that fear is the overriding reason we don't want to stand up to others. We fear being misunderstood. We fear severing the friendship. We fear we'll hurt someone or be so angry we will say something we don't really mean.

Let's face it—confrontation is difficult. Just the thought of approaching someone about a particular issue can send shivers up the spine. But sometimes confrontation is necessary; sometimes it is vital to our healthy relationship with another person. When that is the case, we must confront the person from a basis of love; we call that *caring confrontation*—a part of tough love.

Paul cared enough about those to whom he ministered to challenge them in a caring way. In 1 Thessalonians 2 Paul talks about how he, Silvanus, and Timothy related with the new Christians at Thessalonica:

> Just as you know how we were exhorting and encouraging and imploring each one of you as a father would his own children, so that

you may walk in a manner worthy of the God who calls you into His own kingdom and glory. (1 Thessalonians 2:11–12)

From this passage I want to point out three elements that will help us emulate Paul's style of caring confrontation—the pattern, the process, and the product of his verbal involvement with these people.

THE RIGHT PATTERN

How do we confront others? Paul says he dealt with the Thessalonians as a father would his own children. Earlier, you'll recall, Paul used the metaphor of a nursing mother. I believe the differences are important to note. A nursing mother shows tender love when she cares for and concentrates on nourishing life. We are to respond in the same way to people around us. However, a father is often more involved in instructions and admonitions, superintending the spiritual education of his children. In the same way, as Christian men we are not only to care tenderly for others, but we must also act out of a genuine sense of responsibility for their spiritual edification. Sometimes we must be tough.

Paul also speaks about how he related differently with each person depending upon the state of the individual. He says in 1 Thessalonians 5:14: "And we urge you, brethren, admonish the unruly, encourage the fainthearted, help the weak, be patient with all men."

When we look at the various ways Paul and his coworkers dealt with people in this context, we see their sensitivity. Let's look a little more closely at the four general directions here regarding confronting individuals according to their circumstances.

Admonish the Unruly

The word *unruly,* originally a military term, expressed the character of rebellious soldiers who intentionally disobeyed their superiors and would not stay in their ranks. Apparently in the Thessalonian church some people pulled back on their work because they thought the Lord would come at any moment. Paul says people who shirk their responsibilities are to be warned in the strongest terms.

Encourage the Fainthearted

The term *fainthearted,* also translated 'a melting heart,' refers to those who were despondent about their deceased friends or who were overcome by their own sinfulness. They tended to be highly emotional. They felt defeated by their own sense of personal failure and lacked the spirit to go on with victory in the Christian life. Paul says that such depressed people are not to be admonished but comforted.

Help the Weak

Here Paul is not speaking about the physically weak but the spiritually weak, those who might be afraid of persecution or who are troubled by sin that they cannot overcome. Part of our responsibility is to give weak people emotional and spiritual support. We need to come alongside them and buoy them up. We need to help them sense an accountability to grow. Hebrews 12:12–13 makes this clear:

> Therefore, strengthen the hands that are weak and the knees that are feeble, and make straight paths for your feet, so that the limb which is lame may not be put out of joint, but rather be healed.

This Scripture refers to helping the weak members of the body of Christ.

Be Patient with All Men

The attitude here is one of long suffering in view of the difficulties and problems that are common to all people. Often when we see people who are struggling in areas where we do not, our tendency is to be impatient with them over their rate of spiritual growth. The same impatience carried to an extreme is seen in people who see *any* struggle as unacceptable to God.

Paul speaks strongly against this self-righteous attitude. Don't be surprised when sinners sin. Don't be surprised when people do not gain instant victory in their Christian lives. Instead, realize that it is only by the grace of God that we ourselves make any progress, and we are to extend the same grace toward those around us. We are not to fly off the handle at people or give up on them. We are to work with all people as brothers and sisters in Christ—as people of worth in the sight of God.

Do you see the need for different approaches to different people at different times? Maturity is knowing how to consistently use the right method at the right time with the right person.

THE RIGHT PROCESS

What does "to confront others" mean? Paul uses three different words to explain the process he and his team utilized in confronting the Thessalonians. Those words are *exhorting, encouraging,* and *imploring.*

Exhorting

Paul drew upon the Greek phrase *para kaleo,* which means to 'call alongside.' Exhortation communicates the idea of drawing near to someone, putting your arm around him, and trying to buoy his spirits so that his actions can change. The metaphor is of a general who stands before his troops who have just lost a battle but not the war. The troops are despondent and lack faith in themselves. The general exhorts them and tries to build them up so that their attitudes change. With a more positive attitude, they reenter the battle emboldened.

This concept can be further understood by looking at two aspects of exhortation: complimenting people and expressing confidence in them.

The Power of Compliments

Complimenting is not flattering; when you flatter someone you praise him for qualities over which he has no control, for the purpose of some hidden gain for yourself.

When we rear children, how do we usually compliment them? Think about that for a minute! Usually it is for innate good looks, intelligence, or ability. How often have you heard someone say, "Isn't that a beautiful little baby?" or "Isn't he a smart little guy?"

Dr. James Dobson, an authority on child development, contends that praising children for qualities over which they have no control can have devastating results when those children grow older. They tend to believe that their self-worth is determined only by what they are born with and not at all by what they have done. This leads to a faulty perception of self.

Compliments are proper when given for qualities people are developing in their lives. Jesus praised His men for faith; Paul repeatedly praised believers in the early church for their positive lives of faith.

Everyone desires this type of commendation. William James once said, "The deepest principle of human nature is the craving to be appreciated."

Based on this fact, it appears we need to be giving genuine compliments to people all the time. Since I realized the significance of this, I've tried to say something positive to someone every day. I try to compliment my wife and children and my close friends and associates on a regular basis. My goal is to write a note with a specific compliment to people in my organization on their birthdays or anniversaries or upon the birth of a new child. I might say, "I love you and I appreciate your gentle spirit," or "I appreciate you because of your diligence." Spoken or written compliments carry an almost unimaginable weight. When we make them our habits, the people around us flourish.

The Power of Confidence

The second aspect of exhortation, expressing confidence in people, shows that we trust them not only when they are doing well but also when they make mistakes.

Imagine this. Jesus had poured His life into the twelve disciples. But the night of His arrest, in fear for their own lives, they denied and deserted Him. He suffered the agony of crucifixion along with suffering the humiliation of God's turning away from Him. After He rose from the dead, He appeared to the eleven disciples in the upper room.

Now, what would you have done if you were Jesus? I'll tell you what my natural reaction would have been. I would have let them have it. "It's me! I *told* you I'd be back. But I just stopped by to tell you that you're all out. I don't want anything to do with you. I poured My life into you for three years; I raised the dead, healed the sick, and fed a crowd of 5,000. I told you I was going to die and that I'd be resurrected again, but what did you do? You ran away and hid. Peter, you're the worst—you denied Me three times; you said you didn't even know Me! What kind of a friend is that? You men have failed, and you are *out!*"

Jesus had every right to respond negatively to the lack of faith shown by His disciples. But what did He actually say? "'All authority has been given to Me in heaven and on earth. Go therefore and make disciples of all the nations'" (Matthew 28:18–19). In essence, He declared that He was placing the authority and responsibility for the spiritual outcome of every future generation into the hands of these men—these failures!

You see, Jesus knew how to believe in men. He didn't rub their faces in their failure; instead, He expressed confidence in them.

Howard Hendricks, the great Bible teacher and the man who taught me to communicate, tells a great story of his time in elementary school. Howard says he was such a bad, unruly boy that his fifth-grade teacher had to tie his hands and feet to a chair and gag him.

On the first day of sixth grade, he walked in, saw his new teacher, and heard her say, "So you are Howie Hendricks! I've heard a lot about you!"

Young Howard thought, *Oh no, I'm dead!*

But his new teacher knelt beside him, looked him in the eye, and said, "And I want you to know I don't believe a word of it."

His sixth-grade teacher believed in him from the start. You know what happened? This was a defining moment for that boy, and not only was Howie Hendricks a model student the rest of his school years, but he carried that teacher's confidence with him into his adult life and ministry.

Most people never reach half their potential because no one believes in them. Thus, we can be men of great impact by simply telling and demonstrating to people that we believe in them. If they have failed, we can help them sweep the past behind them. We can tell them we believe they will be used for great things and that they are people of great worth. We can and should verbalize it over and over again until it becomes part of their lives.

Encouraging

The word for *encourage* could be translated as 'support' or 'sustain,' or even 'comfort.' This term is used only three other times in the New Testament, one of which is 1 Thessalonians 5:14. I referred earlier in the chapter to this passage in which Paul talks about encouraging or comforting (uplifting) the faint-hearted.

One role of a real man is that of comforting people in times of need. 2 Corinthians 1:3–4 confirms it:

> Blessed be the God and Father of our Lord Jesus Christ, the Father of mercies and God of all comfort; who comforts us in all our affliction so that we may be able to comfort those who are in any affliction with the comfort with which we ourselves are comforted by God.

We see here that one reason God allows difficulties in our lives is so we can better empathize, understand, and help others in their times of trouble. An illustration of this is recorded in 2 Corinthians 7:5–7:

> For even when we came into Macedonia our flesh had no rest, but we were afflicted on every side: conflicts without, fears within. But God, who comforts the depressed, comforted us by the coming of Titus; and not only by his coming, but also by the comfort with which he was comforted in you, as he reported to us your longing, your mourning, your zeal for me; so that I rejoiced even more.

I hope you get a sense from this passage of the way God wants to use us, as men, to comfort other people. He is looking for us to feel the hurt with people—to empathize with them. And He wants us to be able to show others by our lives how much we love and care for them.

I recall traveling on a plane one morning after an all-night prayer meeting with several hundred pastors in Dallas, Texas. Next to me sat a little girl and her mother. Exhausted, I did not desire any conversation at all. But the mother was very friendly and began to ask me what I did and how I was doing. I explained to her rather transparently that I wasn't feeling all that well. But then God impressed me to try to relate with her because she appeared burdened.

So we began to talk. She told me she was having problems with child rearing, and I tried to understand and empathize without judging her in any way. She became increasingly open. The more I comforted her, the more she talked.

The net result was that after about twenty minutes of my reassuring her in a few rather superficial areas she turned to me and said, "May I tell you something I have never told anyone?" I nodded, and she told me that four months prior to her marriage she had had sexual relations with her husband's boss. She didn't know if her husband knew about it but thought he had for thirteen years.

Can you imagine the guilt that lady carried? She needed love, she needed comfort, and she needed helpful advice. I did what I could to remind her that, though God takes sin seriously, He is a God of love and second chances. I was glad He used me to encourage her, because that's what He wants in a real man's interaction with people. We must know how to "rejoice with those who rejoice, and weep with those who weep" (Romans 12:15).

Imploring

To *implore* means to 'conjure,' or 'to appeal to by something sacred'. Someone else has stated that the term refers to a 'solemn declaration of serious words.'

This concept is found in 1 Thessalonians 4:6, where we read, "And that no man transgress and defraud his brother in the matter because the Lord is the avenger in all these things, just as we also told you before and solemnly warned you."

You can better understand the importance of this concept when you think of your role as a father, if that is applicable, when your child is consistently disobedient. When my son Matt was young he had a pure heart but a very strong will. Mary and I constantly had to work to bring it under the control of the Spirit of God. Sometimes, in tough love, we had to discipline him pretty strongly.

I remember one time when I had to spank Matt repeatedly. I followed each time with the assurance of my love and a discussion of his behavior. Finally, we bowed our heads together and prayed, and Matt asked God to forgive him. Then I put my hand on my heart and asked Matt, "Do you know how much it hurts your daddy and mommy to see you hurt other people? Do you know how much it hurts God?" That was the tender part. I was begging, or imploring, Matt to quit doing bad things. He got the point. People respond when they are implored in the way Paul suggested.

Other New Testament writers further clarify this idea with such words as "refute" (Titus 1:9), "discipline" (Revelation 3:19), and "rebuke" (2 Timothy 4:2). These words communicate seeing a problem in someone's life and trying to restore that person through strong urging.

God encourages us to discern and address problems and sin in the lives of other individuals. But He never intends us to make a judgment in a negative sense about anyone's life. We are not to form quick opinions based on hearsay, talk about others behind their backs, or question people's motives. Nor are we to attack every tiny fault we see. We are to help people by being specific in spelling out serious problems and by offering well-thought-out solutions. We must always keep the person's greatest benefit foremost in our minds.

This concept of admonition is developed in two key passages:

Brethren, even if a man is caught in any trespass, you who are spiritual, restore such a one in a spirit of gentleness; each one looking to yourself, lest you too be tempted. (Galatians 6:1)

"And if your brother sins, go and reprove him in private; if he listens to you, you have won your brother. But if he does not listen to you, take one or two more with you, so that by the mouth of two or three witnesses every fact may be confirmed. And if he refuses to listen to them, tell it to the church; and if he refuses to listen even to the church, let him be to you as a Gentile and a tax-gatherer." (Matthew 18:15–17)

Let me confess another situation in which I really blew it. Some years ago, when I was single, I attended an evangelism conference where I learned how to share my faith. Shortly after the conference I went to the Seafair Torchlight Parade near my hometown in Seattle, Washington. As I walked along the parade route with my date I saw a young man walking up and down in front of the onlookers, passing out religious tracts. He carried a satchel at his side.

As I watched him pass out these tracts I became indignant—he wasn't doing it right! After all, I had just received training in how to share my faith verbally. I thought cramming a tract in someone's face was rude. So I grabbed this man by the shoulder, turned him around, looked him square in the eye and asked, "Why do you cram tracts in people's faces? Don't you know that's rude? Why don't you talk to them?"

Can you guess what he said to me? "Aoaoaoaoa! Aoaoaoaoa!"

He couldn't talk! The poor man had a severe handicap and was unable to speak!

Well, I wanted to crawl into the ground. Eternity passed before me and I saw a great line in heaven. This man stood way up in the front and I was in the very back, with my pants singed. What audacity I had!

I don't want any of my brothers in Christ to make a similar blunder in their attempts to admonish a fellow believer. So, from these passages, let's look briefly at proper admonishment, or how to reprimand others in a humble spirit of Christian love.

First, we are to *admonish the individual privately and personally.* If you have a problem with someone, go directly to him. Don't admonish in a crowd or in front of anyone else. People are naturally embarrassed, humiliated, and even angered when they are confronted publicly. You must speak to the person alone.

Second, we must *admonish prayerfully.* Pray first that God will deal with sin in your own life and make you pure of heart before you approach anyone. Then pray that God will prepare the individual before you talk to him about his problem area, and that God will fill you with wisdom and a humble spirit as you do so.

Third, we must *admonish patiently.* Don't jump all over him! Admonish patiently, calmly, and sensitively because of your love for him.

Fourth, we should *admonish passionately.* By that I mean "with deep feelings." When you see a problem in someone's life, your concern for him must allow you to go to him with sincerity. Be sure you are not flippant or matter-of-fact about what you have to share.

Fifth, we should *admonish positively.* Tell him the positive things you see in his life and how much you appreciate him. Then talk about the one problem you see. Remember, you have an ongoing relationship with this person, and you don't want to communicate in negatives. Assure him that you treasure his positive qualities.

Sixth, we should *admonish practically.* Don't ever just tell someone about a problem in a general sense and leave him hanging. Be specific about the problem, and be ready with a suggestion to help conquer the problem.

Once when I spoke at a conference a young man I didn't know came up to me and declared, "Jenson, I don't like you!"

I said, "I can appreciate that. There probably are many people who don't like me. Tell me what you don't like."

He pondered the issue and retorted, "I don't like anything about you. It's just you!"

"Isn't there anything specific?"

He stopped and thought a moment, then blurted out, "Yeah, it's your personality. I don't like your personality."

"I'm afraid that's not much help. The only way I know to deal with my personality is to shoot myself."

In his clumsy way, this gentleman was trying to admonish me, but he was neither helpful nor practical because he couldn't be specific. Don't confront anyone that way. Give the person some practical handles on what specifically is wrong and how he can deal with the problem.

Seventh, we should *admonish progressively.* Please understand, this one is not for a little disagreement or difference in perspective; rather, it is reserved for a divisive issue or a significant sin. Matthew says that if you go to someone and he doesn't respond to your admonition, then two or more should go with you and talk about it to get clarification. If there is no resolution, then we should take it before the body—the church—or a representation of the church such as the board of elders. If the person still refuses to deal with the problem, he is to be literally excommunicated from the body of believers.

We must care enough to confront when it's necessary. It's not fun, but it's part of being God's man. Personally, my life has been dramatically changed by people who have cared enough to point out my weaknesses to me. Though these situations may have hurt my pride initially, God has used them to build me into more of the kind of man He wants me to be.

THE RIGHT PURPOSE

Why should we confront others? We have looked at the pattern and the process of confrontation, so let's wrap this up by seeing how Paul tells the Thessalonians *why* he confronted them.

His purpose is underscored in 1 Thessalonians 2:12: "So that you may walk in a manner worthy of the God who calls you into His own kingdom and glory."

Paul and his team desired that these people live lives worthy of God. His purpose was to effect a transformation in the hearts of the people. Paul and his colleagues didn't confront others because they themselves were hurt, or angry over a personal offense, or violated or abused, though all of those things had indeed happened to them.

No, they confronted because they cared so deeply. The issue was the spiritual growth of the people…period. When you stop to think about it, that is why God put you and me on this earth: to care deeply for the souls and spiritual growth of others. This means loving a brother so much that we cannot allow a spiritual cancer to fester and grow inside him. We will lovingly confront him, help him excise the cancer, and help him grow strong again.

Real men exercise love for others that is tender when it can be and tough when it must be. We must be committed to helping others live in a manner worthy of the God of the universe.

Action Steps

Identify one person in your life whom you need to confront lovingly. Think through the issue. Work through the seven P approaches listed below and write out your strategy for each. Then go for it!

APPROACH	HOW TO APPLY IT TO THE CHALLENGE
Personally	(e.g., I will speak to Mark personally on Wednesday at Denny's.)
Prayerfully	
Patiently	
Passionately	
Positively	
Practically	
Progressively	

CHAPTER FIFTEEN

Where Do We Go from Here?

A Man after God's Own Heart

The bad news is that our culture is in crisis, much like that of Thessalonica in Paul's day. Personal lives are imploding because people lack the inner resources to make their lives work.

The good news is that we can help restore our disintegrating culture as we encourage men and women to rebuild their lives based on truth. But in order to do so, we must be men who will lead.

We men are becoming increasingly aware of our need to establish biblical priorities. Public opinion analyst Daniel Yankelovich finds that "more than half of American men say that work is no longer their major source of satisfaction." In fact, Yankelovich states,

> Men have come to feel that success on the job is not enough to satisfy their yearnings for self-fulfillment, and they are reaching out for something more and for something different.... The conventional systems no longer satisfy their deepest psychological need nor nourish their self-esteem, nor their cravings for the "full, rich life."[1]

In *The Second Stage,* Betty Friedan offers many examples of men who realize the typical male image cannot answer all their basic needs. And, although the thesis of *The Second Stage* conflicts with my thesis in many ways, it confirms the bankruptcy of secular male typecasting and chronicles a move away from it.

But a move away from any norm carries pain. "Coming out of machismo," Friedan writes, "a man is likely to take a lot of flak, especially from men, and from women who still resist any tradeoff."[2]

These men also may be struggling with their emotions. Friedan quotes an Oakland architect's expression of what dealing with feelings meant to him:

> It makes me feel alive. I exist. I don't feel phony anymore. I don't have to pretend to be so strong because I feel good. I feel centered. The silence that most men live with isolates us, not only from women but from other men. My wife's assault on my silence was, at first, extremely painful. She made me share my feelings with her. It brought an incredible sense of liberation and maybe for the first time in my adult life a sense of reality, that I can feel my feelings and share them with her.
>
> But there'll still be a loneliness, for me and other men, until we can share our feelings with each other. That's what I envy most about the women's movement—the way women share their feelings and the support they get from each other. Do you know how isolated and lonely and weak a man really feels in that silence, never really making contact, never really touching another—man?[3]

Some men are moving toward becoming more open with their feelings. That's great. Many are also seeking to become more effective and positive influences in their homes, churches, and workplaces. I commend them for their efforts.

We have men who would take the lead; as long as there are people to be led, there will be leaders. What we seem not to have, however, is a biblical standard of measurement for an honorable leader.

We cannot expect stable leadership if we allow the changing whims of society to define that leadership. Leaders must be flexible but not flaccid. Michael Macoby, who wrote the bestseller *The Gamesmen* (in which he defined "the leader of the '70s"), also wrote *The Leader,* about "the leader of the '80s." He maintains:

> The old models of leadership no longer work. In an age of individual rights, seductive promises fall flat. In an age of self-expression, even rational authority may seem oppressive. Searching for direction, but critical of anyone who controls us, we look for new leaders as much in fear that we will find them as that we will not.[4]

How can we ever really know what a leader should be apart from the Bible? God's Word is the only constant in our ever-changing world, and unlike secular models, His models of manhood and leadership have stood the test of time. We must draw our definition of a leader from His Word, not only out of obedience to Him but also because His models are immensely practical and effective. The Bible is our absolute guideline because its word is true and its power attainable for all of God's children.

Now What?

You may be asking yourself, "Now what? What do I do with all this information about what a man is? And should I try to be a leader? Compared to Paul, Timothy, and Silvanus, what kind of impact can I have?"

As you look at the state of the world and all the qualities needed in a man, you may feel the end is too far out of sight. But wait! You only need to begin with one step, and then another, building confidence as you go, trusting God with your progress.

Here are my suggestions for where you go from here:

FIRST, believe the urgency of the day.
SECOND, believe that you, as one person, *can* do something.
THIRD, confess your inadequacy to God and accept His forgiveness and empowerment.

And finally, if you have not yet gone to work on the ten core competencies of true manhood and leadership we've studied together, get started today!

Believe the Urgency of the Day

Unless you are convinced that there is, in our day, a particular reason for you to change, you probably won't. The facts are borne out historically. Therefore, you need to be absolutely persuaded that our society is in jeopardy. The four institutions that hold a society together—family, government, business, and religion—are crumbling all around us.

At the heart of the problem is our passivity. We have become morally passive. We have become passive in our marriages and in our families. We have become passive in dealing with the indignities of society. Unless we address this urgent issue quickly, we are doomed. You must believe this in your heart and be passionate about changing it.

Believe That You, As One Person, Can Do Something

Often an individual feels a sense of frustration because he doesn't believe he can have any impact on a situation. You need to know, however, that every one of us can make a difference. Because of the model of your life and through the insights you share with people around you, your society can change.

Whenever God begins to work in a society, He always chooses a man or woman—an individual. He doesn't start with groups; He starts with one person. You need to be convinced of that fact. By yourself, you *can* make a difference.

Confess Your Inadequacy to God and Accept His Forgiveness and Empowerment

Permit me to address you man to man on this issue. Guys have a big struggle in this area. After all, "How can I be a leader when I blow it so much? I'm a horrible model!"

Remember, the point here is not that we be perfect. No one is! And we Christians won't be until we meet the Lord in heaven. We do need to pursue perfection, but watch out! We can run into a tremendous snare. So often Christian men who step out and try to grow get caught here.

Imagine this scenario: You attended a big Promise Keepers stadium event. God touched you deeply, and you made a real commitment to be a Promise Keeper.

You came home and began to meet with several other guys in an accountability group. This was great. With high enthusiasm the guys supported you and began to see you as a growing leader. Then something started to happen.

The enthusiasm began to melt away and some old habits reared their ugly heads. You lost your temper, watched some things you shouldn't have on TV, slipped up in your times with the Lord. Your fresh commitment to your wife and children began to take a back seat again to your work.

To increase the problem, you are now seen as a Promise Keeper at church, so you are expected to shine as an example. What do you do?

I believe many men face this dilemma today. You made an honest commitment but you simply don't have the resources, support, or wisdom to continue.

Don't just "fake it till you make it" or put on a false face. This is deadly legalism and God hates it. The Pharisees did this. They pretended they were super saints, keeping all the laws. But in their religious fervor they lost the spirit of God's love.

And don't you believe for a minute that your pastor or any other saint has it all together. They don't. I certainly don't. I blow it every day—we all do.

Remember, one of the keys to the successful Christian life is not to pretend to be perfect, but to progress toward the likeness of Christ. Paul told Timothy his progress should be evident to all (1 Timothy 4:15).

So how do you move toward a Christ-honoring life? You endeavor to "abide in Christ and let His Word abide in you" every part of every day. When you blow it (sin), simply confess that sin (agree with God that it is sin) and experience God's forgiveness.

You will fall into the mud (sin) periodically, but you don't need to live in it. The godly man has learned how to get back up quickly and "walk in the light" again. He gets his relationship with God cleansed whenever it has been sullied.

Your best modeling may be to let people see how you handle your failures. Think about that!

In fact, as you've seen in this book, whenever I write or speak I try to share some negative illustration about myself. Why? you may wonder. Well, two reasons. First, I have so much material to draw from! And second, I want people to know it is okay to blow it sometimes.

People who hear these stories don't think, *What a creep he is.* Instead they think, *Wow, he is like me, yet he seems to be doing all right. Maybe there is hope for me too.* And, my friend, we all need hope.

Two Extremes

Too many of us experience one of two extremes when it comes to facing our sinfulness. At one extreme a person becomes so preoccupied with his falling short of God's mark that he is immobilized. That is a strategy of Satan. If he can get you to believe you are worthless, he has won the battle.

However, 1 John 1:9 assures us, "If we confess our sins, He is faithful and righteous to forgive us our sins and to cleanse us from all unrighteousness." We are forgiven unconditionally. God knows we are sinful and is not surprised when we do sin, but the burden is on Him to guide us away from a sinful lifestyle.

At the other extreme is the person who sins but overlooks it. He simply does not admit that he is less than what God desires. This kind of behavior springs from a fear of admitting failure and being rejected. You need to know that it is okay to admit you are sinful. Be honest as you look at yourself. Confess to God where you have been inadequate. Once you have identified your mistakes and confessed them, you can claim God's forgiveness. Do not be immobilized by guilt.

Plug in to the God of the Universe

Of course, everything we've discussed in our time together is moot if you have not yet received Jesus Christ as your personal Savior and Lord. So it really begins with being sure you are properly plugged in to the God of the universe. If you have never come to know Jesus Christ as your Savior, I urge you to do so right now. Simply turn to Him in prayer and say:

Lord Jesus, I need You. I know I am sinful and therefore separated from God. And I realize You died on the cross to pay the penalty for my sin. Right now I ask You to come into my life and to make me the kind of person You want me to be.

If you sincerely prayed that prayer, or have prayed one similar to it in the past, you can be sure that Christ has come into your life. God's Holy Spirit enters into us and gives us the desire to do what God wants us to do. He also gives us the power to accomplish it (see Philippians 2:12–13). Make sure Christ is ruling in your life. If you hold back any area from His complete control, He will not have the freedom to move and you won't have the power to become a real man.

Commit to Growing the Core Competencies

In addition to depending upon God's Holy Spirit to empower and change you, you need to plan for and move toward the development of the ten core competencies we've looked at in this book. Let me suggest how you can build these qualities into your life one by one.

1. Start memorizing 1 Thessalonians 2:7–12 to give yourself a biblical basis for your actions.

2. Go over this summarized list of the ten core competencies we've studied together. Evaluate yourself as to where you are today in each of them (2 = weak; 8 = strong).

A team orientation	2 4 6 8
A disciplined life	2 4 6 8
Gentleness	2 4 6 8
The freedom to be affectionate	2 4 6 8
The ability to communicate effectively	2 4 6 8
Openness and honesty	2 4 6 8
A willingness to serve	2 4 6 8
The desire to work hard	2 4 6 8
Holiness	2 4 6 8
The ability to confront	2 4 6 8

3. Evaluate the quality of your biblical manhood and leadership in your personal life, your marriage and family, your social life, and your involvement in church, ministry, and business. What lack do you find in these areas? What changes need to be made?

4. Review this book, concentrating on the core competencies one at a time. If you fall short in the area of gentleness, for example, you can focus on that quality. Think through and meditate upon a passage of Scripture relevant to the specific quality you want to develop. Do this at least four times a day. I recommend that when you get up in the morning, you spend five to ten minutes just meditating on these. Then again around lunchtime, around dinnertime, and before you go to bed. Bring these competencies before the Lord in prayer, emphasizing the one you are focusing on.

5. If you find yourself failing, don't quit! Growth takes time. Just as it took time for you to develop the habit of not doing certain things, it takes time for you to acquire and practice a new habit. Therefore, continue with each specific area through meditation and discipline every day for at least twenty-one days. Let that be your goal—and it will prove a significant building block in your growth.

6. As suggested before, keep a journal or write a "Dear Jesus" letter every day. Write down how you are doing. Record your failures and your successes, and hold yourself accountable to your own goal of becoming a stronger man of God.

7. Finally, make yourself accountable to someone else. Be open and honest enough to tell your wife or a friend what you are trying to do. Have this person ask you daily how you are doing. Ask him or her to pray for you and to encourage you in every possible way. This accountability will keep you honest and help you grow.

The point of all this is to give God the opportunity to build these ten core competencies into your life. Trust Him to build them in as you discipline yourself and practice biblical meditation. If you do this, God will begin to move you toward becoming a man after His own heart. In addition, as you begin to take the lead, your changed life will begin to change those around you and, in turn, our desperately needy society.

Remember, ours is an urgent day. Be sure, therefore, to keep your priorities straight—for if you were to win the whole world and lose your own soul, what worth would it be? What profit would it be for you? If you were to be very successful in business and yet not be the man God wants you to be, how valuable would that be?

God holds us accountable for each day of our lives. We cannot hold back for any reason. You have seen the problem and the biblical solution. God is waiting for you to trust and follow Him, as David did, and as Paul, Timothy, and Silvanus did. Now the rest is up to you. Reflect on the following poem as you begin the application of these leadership skills.

> I counted dollars, while God counted crosses.
> I counted gains, while He counted losses.
> I counted my worth by things gained in store.
> He sized me up by the scars that I bore.
> I coveted honors and sought degrees.
> He wept while He counted the hours on my knees.
> I never knew until one day by the grave,
> How vain are the things that we spend life to save.
>
> author unknown

Action Steps

In the power of God's Spirit, go to work on the suggestions in this chapter for applying what we've discussed together. Before God and your accountability team, commit to growing the ten core competencies of Christian manhood and leadership in your life.

Study
and
Discussion
Guide

Manhood in the Making

This study and discussion guide will help you apply the principles of each chapter of *Taking the Lead*. Although you can use it for private study, I believe you'll find it much more effective if you work through it with other men.

Please review the appropriate chapter of the book before delving into its corresponding session of the study guide. These sessions will help you MULL (think about and discuss) the key issues of each chapter. You will find suggested Scriptures to MEMORIZE, positive habits to MASTER, and a guided prayer to MEDITATE upon as you move toward true manhood.

Enjoy the journey!

CHAPTER ONE

Christian Men Wanted!

Mull

- State the problem as it applies to you and discuss how you can find the motivation to change.
- Discuss the three attributes of a healthy church and how your help can strengthen the spirit of unity in your own church.
- Think through the reflection question under the Action Steps at the end of the chapter. Review your evaluations and your answers to the questions throughout the chapter.
- Be sure to complete the last activity that builds your action steps into your calendar for the week.

Memorize

- Take five minutes right now to commit 1 Thessalonians 2:7 to memory. If you are with a group, pair up and practice with one another. During the next week, get it down cold. (Tips for memorizing: Write the verse on a small card and carry it with you. Read it and say it 25 times the first day, 20 times the second day, 15 times the third day, etc. Within a week it should be a part of you.)

Master

- Commit the ten core competencies of leadership from 1 Thessalonians 2:7–12 to memory. Get these down for next week. They will become the grid through which you can build an effective ministry at home, church, and work.

MEDITATE

Gracious Lord, thank You for not giving me what I deserve, but for loving me out of Your grace. I am so thankful for that! I know I have failed to be the leader You want me to be in my home, church, business, and community; I now commit to change.

As I seek to build the ten core competencies into my life in the days to come, I'll depend upon You for the power, insight, and motivation needed to make the changes necessary. I'll "put off the old man" (bad habits) and "put on the new man" (good habits) as I discipline myself "for the purpose of godliness" as You command in 1 Timothy 4:7. Help me as I determine to develop real manhood.

And, Lord, I'll not allow Satan to immobilize me through fear, shame, or defeat. I won't let him rob me of the joy You have for me and the impact on others that You want to flow through me. I am Yours. Mold me and use me for Your glory and Kingdom. Amen.

CHAPTER TWO

Building Biblical Brotherhood

Mull

- State from memory the ten core competencies of leadership from 1 Thessalonians 2:7–12.
- If in a group (you should be!), discuss the exercise dealing with identifying a close friend and then listing the ways you know you can count on him. What did you come up with? Talk about it.
- Consider obtaining some FIRO B tests and taking them together as a group. Discuss the results.
- Do you agree or disagree that "relationships are vital" from a scriptural perspective? Why?
- Discuss the four levels of relationships listed. Then share what you filled in on the table that describes the types of relationships you have with your friends. How would you like to improve your situation with each person listed?
- Discuss the two action steps suggestions. Be honest!

Memorize

- Take a few minutes to pair up and check each other out on the verse you memorized last week, 1 Thessalonians 2:7; then add 1 Thessalonians 2:8. This will show you that you can memorize Scripture.

Master

- Practice being a committed friend to one other man. Concentrate, focus, and build being supportive into a new, improved habit with that person. Once you master this, you can utilize this skill with others.

Meditate

Lord, thank You for my friends! I long to take our relationships to a deeper level and to be a better friend myself. But You know how selfish I can get. Please, Lord, get me out of myself. Let me focus on being their friend, instead of expecting them to be my friends.

Teach me the power of Philippians 2:3–4 where Paul says in effect, "In humility of mind I am to esteem others as more important than myself. I'm not to look at life just from my own perspective but also through the eyes of others."

Man, that's tough. But make it so, dear Father. Make it so. Amen.

Building Your Team

Mull

- With the group, share from memory 1 Thessalonians 2:7–8. I know this seems difficult, but remember that according to Psalm 119:9–11 the key to purity (and personal growth for that matter) is Scripture memory and meditation. Read that passage. (Better yet, memorize it—especially verse 11.)
- List the six qualities of committed relationships from this chapter. Then unpack and try to explain at least one of them.
- Share your evaluations and insights from the Servant Quality chart at the end of principle 1.
- Share your answers to the questions at the end of principle 2.
- Finally, focus on the Action Steps. Articulate your strengths and weaknesses as well as your action step.
- Don't let this action step slip. Discuss ways your team members can intensify their support for each other.

Memorize

- Add verse 9 to 1 Thessalonians 2:7–8.

Master

- Choose one of the six principles and begin to put it to work. Remember, practice, practice, practice. If you give yourself twenty-one days of consistent practice, you can build a habit into your life. Then you don't have to think about it a great deal. You just need to apply it. So practice. Choose one and stay on it until it becomes part of you.

MEDITATE

Wow! Lord, I am so impressed with the team relationship David and Jonathan had. I want the same with a brother or two. Let me take the initiative and not just wait for someone else to pursue me. Let me serve as freely and generously as Jonathan did when he served David, with nothing expected in return. Keep reminding me that the way to lead is to serve, and the way to get ahead is to be last, and that if I love my friends, they'll be motivated to love me. Thank You for the team we have and for the support and love for each other that You are developing in us.

Thank You for building new skills into my life. I believe that You will fashion me by the power of Your Spirit. I need Your power, great God, and I will trust in the fact that "I can do all things through Him who strengthens me" (Philippians 4:13). Amen.

CHAPTER FOUR

Power in Control
Part One

Mull

- Complete and discuss the evaluation on discipline in the beginning of the chapter. Identify the weakest area in your life.
- Talk through the three major qualities of discipline (pain, focus, and perseverance in habit formation). Share some examples from your life.
- Memorize the HABIT acrostic and practice sharing it.
- Carefully think through establishing a plan for discipline, and complete the exercises at the end of the chapter to flesh out your plan. Share your plan with someone else for the sake of accountability.

Memorize

- Make 1 Timothy 4:7 and 12 your own.

Master

- Every day for twenty-one days, practice the discipline plan you developed. Remember, positive habit development will give you great power and freedom.

MEDITATE

Lord, let me be a proper example in speech, conduct, love, faith, and purity as You described in 1 Timothy 4:12. Instead of pretending to be perfect or trying to project some false image, teach me to go deeper with You and let You build these desirable qualities into my life.

I will trust You to empower me as I discipline myself for the purpose of godliness. I'll work out what You are working in me. Amen.

CHAPTER FIVE

Power in Control
Part Two

Mull

- Repeat to someone the elements in the HABIT acrostic and then explain and discuss the four covered in this chapter, one at a time, following these suggestions:
- What is meant by "allowing God's power to work"? Explain it simply as you would to a child. Particularly reveal the difference between God's part in your growth and your part. Discuss the chart at the end of that section of the chapter.
- Explain "building an accountability structure." How do you do that? Discuss the importance of such a structure, and how you want your accountability structure to work in your life.
- Talk about how you can use journaling here, and about counting the cost.
- Think about the Consequences Catalog and do the exercises recommended here.
- What role does "internalizing God's Word" play? How does it help you keep your own power under control? Discuss meditation and the function it has in this process. Explain the "memorize, mull, and mind" process to someone. Keep it simple.
- Finally, describe the process of "training consistently." How do you do it?
- Complete the exercises at the end of the chapter, specifically spelling out how you plan to put the five HABIT principles to work.

Remember, practice, practice, practice—practice the same activity for twenty-one straight days to make it a habit, thereby disciplining yourself "for the purpose of godliness."

MEMORIZE

- Put Joshua 1:8 and Philippians 4:8 into your memory bank.

MASTER

- Get the HABIT acrostic down cold. Be able to say it from memory and to explain it. Practice it for twenty-one straight days. You can utilize this method in many ways in the days to come. It will provide the needed tools for you to gain and maintain discipline. And, hey, you can even pass it on to your family and friends.

MEDITATE

Father, this area of power control is so tough. I'm constantly shocked at the areas in my life where I struggle. It seems I have carried so many old bad habits into my present life from my early childhood and teenage years. Why?

I guess I know the answer. I carried the sin bent with me even when I gave my life to You. But now, You desire to bring me into conformity to Your heart and will. As I grow from "glory to glory into Your likeness," I know I'll become more like You and less like the world. I realize it's a process.

And Lord, I won't give up! I understand discipline involves pain, focus, and perseverance, and so I will take two steps forward and, sometimes, a step back. But I know I am forgiven and I know that You empower me to "discipline myself for godliness."

Today I choose to be Your man. By Your power and the encouragement and support of the brothers, I'll "press on toward the goal" You have for me—conformity to the likeness of Your Son. Amen.

CHAPTER SIX

Gentle, Not Timid

Mull

- Pair up for five minutes and check each other out on the two Scripture memory verses from the last session (Joshua 1:8 and Philippians 4:8), and 1 Thessalonians 2:7–9.
- Articulate what gentleness is not and discuss how those misperceptions do or do not reflect your own bias.
- Discuss the four attributes of gentleness.
- Interact on your specific plan to put gentleness to work this week based on the final action step at the end of the chapter.

Memorize

- Start committing 1 Thessalonians 5:14 to memory today.

Master

- Put your plan to work this week per the final action step in the chapter. Practice, practice, practice gentleness. Remember, this is a learned habit. As you practice it, you will begin to feel it.

Meditate

Lord, I'm sorry that I get so angry at people sometimes. What astounds me is how I can get the angriest at those closest to me—my kids, my wife, my friends. Lord, I give my "violated rights" back to You. I know I am to live as a servant with no rights but with many responsibilities. I have chosen to follow that path and I follow it gladly.

Therefore, empower me by Your Spirit to be gentle the way Jesus was. I know this isn't weakness but controlled strength. Let me die to self and help me treat others as fragile, needy people. I feel they deserve less; let me give them more. Lord, I'm just so thankful that You are gentle with me and don't give me what I deserve, but give me an abundant life out of Your grace. Therefore, I choose to treat others as You treat me. Amen.

CHAPTER SEVEN

The Power of Affection
Part One

Mull

- Share 1 Thessalonians 5:14 from memory. Discuss how you were able to apply it this past week.
- Share your victories and failures on "applying gentleness" this past week. What are you learning?
- Summarize the six steps toward fond affection listed in this chapter. Which ones are you best at? Which ones are the hardest for you?
- Particularly focus on the issue of bitterness. Have you forgiven all the people who have hurt you in your past? What about your dad? Your mom? Be sure to process this one and apply what you are asked to do in this chapter.
- Share your responses to the action steps at the end of the chapter.

Memorize

- The six steps to building powerful affection: feel positive emotions, think positive thoughts, focus on the positive in people, offer positive prayers, speak positive words, and practice positive emotions.

Master

- Practice the assignment in the closing action step of the chapter. Build your action steps into your calendar (e.g., when will you say that affectionate word or carry out that affectionate act?). Remember, "faith without works is dead." So go to work!

MEDITATE

Father, I hurt! I feel that I was unjustly treated when _____ did _____ to me. It wasn't fair. I didn't deserve it. I suffered.

But now I know, in part, why. No one ever suffered like You, Lord Jesus. Yet You did not react when You went to the cross. You just kept entrusting Yourself to the Father. You knew the Father had a plan. And in accordance with that plan, it is by Your wounds that I have been healed.

Now I can help others to be healed as I respond lovingly and with forgiveness even when I am mistreated. In fact, You say I have been called for this very purpose. So I choose to forgive. I will not allow bitterness to rest in me. I give it to You. And as You have forgiven me, so I will forgive others. Right now I forgive _____.

And I choose to love with intensity. I will think, feel, and act as You do toward me—with overwhelming care and affection. Amen.

CHAPTER EIGHT

The Power of Affection
Part Two

Mull

- Review the six steps toward fond affection.
- Report on your success and/or failure this past week in applying this skill. Hey, be honest. Remember, you don't need to pretend to be perfect. You are simply trying to learn and progress.
- Talk through the assignment to focus on ten positive qualities in someone. Share your list.
- Interact on the assignment to evaluate your own communication style. Review the chart on positive versus negative comment percentages.
- Discuss your responses to the action steps at the end of the chapter.

Memorize

- First Corinthians 13:4–7. I know, I know. This is tough. But this is a classic passage on love. You will be working on it for several sessions, but start getting it down now.

Master

- Put your action step to work. Remember, you must practice it as you discipline yourself "for the purpose of godliness." Discipline takes time. Each day you need to put these skills to work. So plan your work and then work your plan—daily.

MEDITATE

Lord, I love the world; it's just people I can't stand sometimes. I just want to go into my cave and hide. I get so filled up with people that I think I am suffocating. Help me!

Let me see people the way You see them—needy, broken, hurt, special, filled with potential, created in Your image. Let me see through Your eyes and feel with Your heart. Then I can love with Your love.

Flow Your affection toward others through me. I can't love the way You can, but I can allow Your power to work through me. I am Yours—use me! Amen.

CHAPTER NINE

EFFECTIVE COMMUNICATION

MULL

- Go around the group, each man saying from memory as much of the 1 Corinthians 13:4–7 passage as he can. Encourage each other!
- Share your victories and setbacks on the assignment for the last session. How are you changing? What progress do you see? What is God teaching you? Share the insights you have gained and the comments you have heard from those around you.
- Give your own definition for "effective communication." How well do you do at it?
- Review the nine vital principles for effective communication from this chapter. Which one is your greatest strength? your greatest weakness? Give a recent example. Be vulnerable here. Remember, we are all in process.
- Share your insights from the action steps assignment. Explain your plan.

MEMORIZE

- Commit to memory the nine vital principles for effective communication. These will help you! Get them into yourself. Then put them to work. Also continue memorizing 1 Corinthians 13:4–7.

MASTER

- Choose one person toward whom you can apply these nine skills this week (try your spouse or a close friend). Then think through the skills several times a day and carefully apply them. If you "fall off the horse," get right back on. Remember, discipline is painful at times but very rewarding when a skill becomes a habit. And if you can master clear communication, you will be a big winner.

MEDITATE

Oh, great God, I am so often guilty of not applying the truths in this chapter. I normally want others to understand me much more than I want to understand them. Change me here. Let me seek first to understand and then to be understood. Let me listen more and talk less—with others and with You.

Empower me to watch my tongue. How many times I have opened my mouth and said words that hurt! Show me how to be sensitive and loving with nonverbals as well—my tone, my eye contact, my body language.

I need a lot of help, precious Father. I am Your man and want to reflect Your character. So please make me effective and loving in my communication. Amen.

CHAPTER TEN

Giving Your Life

Mull

- Review 1 Thessalonians 2:8 and 1 Corinthians 13:4–7. What has God been saying to you in these areas the past few weeks?
- Discuss your progress in effective communication this week. How did you do? What is the funniest thing that happened to you in this area?
- Summarize the three core skills involved in giving your life.
- Share your answers to the seven questions about openness asked in this chapter. What insights about yourself did you gain here?
- Talk through your self-evaluation based on the exercise regarding the percentage of time you spend with others at the clichés, gossip, opinions, feelings, and complete honesty levels. What did you learn about your relationships? What do you need to do to improve?
- Talk further about your openness evaluation in response to the action steps at the end of the chapter.

Memorize

- Complete your memorization of 1 Corinthians 13:4–7. If you have finished this passage, then review it. This is the last week to work on this passage and get it down pat.

Master

- This week, launch your strategy to be more transparent. This will be a tough one. Most of us guys just aren't good in this area. Remember, though, your goal is not to pretend to be perfect but to make progress. That phrase will set you free if you can embrace it. It's okay not to be perfect. None of us is. You free others up to progress themselves when you choose to admit your own vulnerability.

Meditate

Lord, I am afraid to tell others who I am. They might not like me if they really knew me. Yet You tell me in Your Word that if I "walk in the light as He is in the light," I can have true fellowship with You and with others. You know my sin and still You embrace me. But will others? I need Your help with that fear.

I do believe You, Father. So I'll open up. Show me how. Show me when and where. Give me some friends who will love me just as I am—flawed but seeking to grow into Your likeness.

Let me experience a new level of intimacy with You and others as I impart not just the gospel (truth) but my very own life (my inner soul). Amen.

CHAPTER ELEVEN

Strength in Servanthood

Mull

- Review the two core competencies focused on in this chapter on servant leadership. Which one are you best at? Why?
- Discuss what humility is not as described in this chapter. In your opinion, how have these misconceptions become part of the typical male worldview?
- Discuss what humility is as described in this chapter. How humble do you perceive yourself to be? Be honest!
- State the qualities of sacrificial giving listed in this chapter. Which one do you struggle with the most? Can you give a recent example? Ask the group how you can make that aspect easier for yourself.
- Share your answers to the action steps questions.

Memorize

- Commit Philippians 4:13 to memory. Start today.

Master

- Enter the plan of action you wrote in response to the action steps into your schedule right now—when, where, with whom, and how you will put it to work. Then begin working that plan. Remember, you're "putting on" the new man as you build your own godly habits.

MEDITATE

A servant? Lord, I am anything but a servant! The fact of the matter is, I don't want to serve my wife, my children, or my friends, and certainly not just the average Joe. I want to be served. I want others to meet my needs. I want to receive, not give. I want my way, not someone else's way. I want to be first, not last.

I guess that is in no small measure why You came and died for me—I'm so innately selfish. So today let me live in Your humility, realizing I still carry those sin habits, for it is only "through Christ who strengthens me" that I can overcome them. Therefore, I'll attempt to stay broken, yielded, and pliable in Your hands.

At the same time, I will also embrace the reality that "I can do all things." You have said I am special. You have forgiven me, loved me, chosen me, and ordained me to reflect Your glory. Therefore, I will walk with my head high, understanding that You have chosen me to be a kingdom rep, to make a difference. Wherever I go I'll represent You and the principles of Your kingdom.

And I'll do it Your way—by sacrificially giving of myself that others might truly live. Through Your power, I'll be a servant. Make it so, Lord. Make it so! Amen.

CHAPTER TWELVE

WORKING HARD

MULL

- Review your memory work on Philippians 4:13. How did you do at putting this verse to work this week?
- What opportunity did you take to live as a servant/leader since the last session? What were the circumstances? What did you do? How did it make you feel?
- Review 1 Thessalonians 2:7–9 from memory.
- State the four main things to remember in this chapter on hard work. Which is the hardest for you?
- Talk about how Paul's life illustrates the section "Life Is Tough." Does your life reflect these same areas of struggle? Illustrate from something that happened during the past month.
- Discuss what you wrote in response to the action steps instructions. Explain your plan. Remember, you must always move toward action. If you just learn these truths intellectually, you will find that your "pride in knowledge" will tend to puff you up. Instead, let God transform you by empowering you in these new skills.

MEMORIZE

- Second Corinthians 4:16–18. This is a great text on the right perspective to have toward life.

MASTER

- Put the action step to work.

MEDITATE

How often I get frustrated and overwhelmed with my circumstances, Father. I am such a wimp at times. When I see how Paul and the disciples suffered or think of the persecuted church today, I am stunned at my own softness.

Lord, don't let me be soft. Let me, instead, toughen up, be strong, be courageous, not quit. Make my true manhood real. Let me know the resurrection power of Christ, not just when I am in a ministry setting but also in every other moment of my life—when I feel like punching out a guy at work for something he says, when I am doing "gofer" work that I don't think I deserve, when I am confronted with obstacles and challenges in my personal life.

Dear Father, regardless of the circumstances, let me be Your man of steel. Let me focus on the roots and allow You to take care of growing Your fruit in and through me. I commit to renewing myself daily as I spend time in Your Word, prayer, fellowship, rest, reflection, planning, and growing. I'll stay a sharpened ax in Your hand. Use me! Amen.

CHAPTER THIRTEEN

A Winning Lifestyle

Mull

- Review from memory 2 Corinthians 4:16–18. Describe the impact those verses may have had on your life this week. Where were you able to put them to work?
- State the three main elements of holiness listed in this chapter and explain how they lead to a winning lifestyle.
- Discuss the Scriptures dealt with under the Power of Example section. Which one grabs your attention the most? How have you seen the power of your own example on others or others on you?
- What three aspects of "example" does Paul address as illustrations? Which is your greatest challenge?
- Talk about the role personal forgiveness plays in being an example, and why.
- How well have you succeeded at "putting off" and "putting on" based on the chart from Colossians 3?
- Discuss how you responded to the instructions in the action steps section.
- Read the entire text of Longfellow's poem printed at the beginning of this book.

Memorize

- First John 1:9 and 1 Thessalonians 2:10.

Master

- Practice this week the power of 1 John 1:9 as described in action steps. Keep "short accounts" with God by confessing your sins as the Holy

Spirit convicts you, and experience God's forgiveness. Satan wants you defeated and in the dark, but God wants you in the light. It's your choice which voice to follow.

MEDITATE

Abba, Father, can I really be an example? I feel so unworthy. I've messed up so much in my life. Am I truly forgiven? Am I truly able to lead others? Won't I be a hypocrite?

Or is it really true that You have totally forgiven me? You want to keep me reconciled with You. You want me to walk in Your Spirit and live in the light with my sins confessed to You, in humble obedience and faith so I can progress into Your likeness "from glory to glory." Help me to model godly progression rather than pretending to have a godly perfection.

Keep me in the light, Father. Let me not "fake it till I make it," but simply progressively grow into Your perfect image by the power of Your Spirit. Amen.

CHAPTER FOURTEEN

TOUGH LOVE, TENDER LOVE

MULL

- Review 1 John 1:9 and 1 Thessalonians 2:10 and share with the group what God has taught you this week from these Scriptures.
- What kind of example were you this past week? Where did you blow it? Where did you advance?
- Discuss the four steps to appropriate confrontation under "The Right Pattern" section of this chapter. How well do you do at adjusting your conflict resolution to the needs of the other person? Share an example of your growth in this area.
- Talk about the differences regarding exhorting, encouraging, and imploring as described in "The Right Process" section. Which one is the hardest for you? Why?
- Explain how the "right purpose" is vital in caring confrontation.
- Review your answers to the action steps. Walk through what you will do specifically this week.

MEMORIZE

- First Thessalonians 2:11–12

MASTER

- Follow the procedures you listed in the action steps for the person you identified. Now work at making this a habit on all issues. Begin building consistency into your life.

MEDITATE

Lord God, I am uncomfortable about confronting others. I don't know if it is because I am fearful of rejection, unaccustomed to doing this, unaware of how to do it, or sense my own inadequacies so much that I feel hypocritical identifying the "speck" in my brother's eye.

I suppose all of the above is true. Regardless, You urge me to care enough to confront appropriately—not just to admonish but also to encourage, lift up, support, and be a true friend. Lord, I confess my own selfishness here and turn to You for Your supernatural love. Help me to lovingly help others to become all You want them to be. Amen.

CHAPTER FIFTEEN

WHERE DO WE GO FROM HERE?

MULL

- Review 1 Thessalonians 2:11–12 from memory. Go ahead and recite it! Share together what impact Scripture memorization has had on you during the past few months.
- Talk through the "Now What?" section. Discuss the four steps suggested and how you can help one another continue to grow in the areas you've been discussing.
- Discuss the section titled "Commit to Growing the Core Compentencies." Talk about the importance of the exercises here—all seven of them.

MEMORIZE

- Review the memorization work you've done during your study of *Taking the Lead:* the Scripture verses, the ten core competencies of leadership, the HABIT acrostic.

MASTER

- Keep the ten core competencies in your memory bank and build them consistently into your life. Let these become the grid through which you flesh out your own Christian manhood and leadership in the days to come. Let them expand your effectiveness in your home, church, and workplace.

MEDITATE

Wow, Lord! Where do I begin? There is so much to do and I feel so inadequate. But You know that. In fact, I know it is good news to You that I realize I am inadequate. That means Your power can "be made perfect through my weakness" as I depend upon You.

Make me Your kind of man, my gracious God, a man after Your own heart. Mold me into Your likeness. Rule over me. Fill me with Your Spirit and keep me soft and pliable. I know I'll fail daily, but I also know Your grace is sufficient and You will transform me as I stay rooted in Your Word and controlled by Your Spirit.

I am Your man. Make me a servant/leader like Paul, Timothy, and Silvanus. And, dear Father, give me others with whom I can be a co-laborer in Your work.

I love You! Amen.

A Parting Word

My brother, I know I have given you a great deal to handle. But remember, God is in the business of forming you into His image. And that is a life-long process. So be patient. Take one skill at a time and turn it into a habit. Let God continue to mold you and make you into the man He wants you to be. You are His man, created by Him for a mighty work, beginning in your own home and personal life and moving into your church, workplace, and community.

God has called you for such a time as this. He believes in you. I believe in you. Now I want *you* to believe in you and what our great God can do through you.

May God bless you, my friend. I've enjoyed our time together, and I look forward to seeing what God does in and through you in the days to come.

For further information about Dr. Jenson's training programs
and products, contact him at:

Dr. Ron Jenson, chairman
Future Achievement International
12989 Abra Drive
San Diego, California 92128

phone: (619) 487–3177
fax: (619) 487–9212
futureone@earthlink.net

NOTES

CHAPTER TWO
BUILDING BIBLICAL BROTHERHOOD

1. John Powell, *Why Am I Afraid to Tell You Who I Am?* (Chicago, Ill.: Argus communications, 1969), 43.

CHAPTER FIVE
POWER IN CONTROL, PART TWO

1. Henry T. Blackaby and Claude V. King, *Experiencing God Workbook* (Nashville, Tenn.: LifeWay Press, 1990).

CHAPTER SIX
GENTLE, NOT TIMID

1. J. Oswald Sanders, *Spiritual Leadership* (Chicago: Moody Press, 1980), 63.

CHAPTER EIGHT
THE POWER OF AFFECTION, PART TWO

1. Quoted in *For Dads Only,* January 1980.
2. Jack Mayhall and Carole Mayhall, *Marriage Takes More Than Love* (Colorado Springs, Colo.: NavPress, 1996).

CHAPTER NINE
EFFECTIVE COMMUNICATION

1. AutoCover (Hampshire, England, n.d.).
2. H. Norman Wright, *Communication: Key to Your Marriage* (Glendale, Calif.: Regal Books, 1974), 54.

CHAPTER TEN
GIVING YOUR LIFE

1. Paul Tournier, *The Meaning of Persons* (Cutchoque, N.Y.: Buccaneer Books, 1993).
2. James Dolby, *I, Too, Am Man.*

CHAPTER ELEVEN
STRENGTH IN SERVANTHOOD

1. Charles R. Swindoll, *Improving Your Serve* (Nashville, Tenn.: Word Publishing, 1990), 15.
2. Some material in this section is adapted with the permission of Bruce Narramore from *You're Someone Special* (Grand Rapids, Mich.: Zondervan Publishing House, 1980).
3. Swindoll, 42.
4. Alexander Whyte, *Bible Characters,* Vol. 2, The New Testament (London: Oliphants Ltd., 1952), 190.

CHAPTER TWELVE
WORKING HARD

1. H. Homes and R. H. Rahe, "The Social Readjustment Rating Scale," from *Journal of Psychosomatic Research,* Vol. 11 (New York, N.Y.: Pergamon Press, Ltd., 1967).

CHAPTER THIRTEEN
A WINNING LIFESTYLE

1. *Signs of the Times* (Rockville, Md.: Assurance Publishers, 1979), 326.
2. Ibid., 617.
3. Ibid.

CHAPTER FIFTEEN
WHERE DO WE GO FROM HERE?

1. David Yankelovich, quoted by Betty Friedan in *The Second Stage* (New York: Summit Books, 1981), 134.
2. Friedan, 152.
3. Ibid., 154.
4. Michael Macoby, *The Leader* (New York: Simon & Schuster, 1981), 17.